How to See the British Museum in Four Visits

W. Blanchard Jerrold

Contents

INTRODUCTION. 7
FOUR DISTINCT VISITS. 11
VISIT THE FIRST. 11
VISIT THE SECOND. 50
VISIT THE THIRD. 91
VISIT THE FOURTH. 129
NOTES 164

HOW TO SEE THE BRITISH MUSEUM IN FOUR VISITS

BY

W. Blanchard Jerrold

INTRODUCTION.

The money to found a British Museum was raised by a lottery in the middle of the last century. Sir Hans Sloane having offered his books and museum of natural history to Parliament, for less than half its value (20,000L.), it was purchased, together with the famous Harleian and Cottonian MSS., and deposited in Montague House, Bloomsbury, which had been bought of the Earl of Halifax, for the sum of 10,250L. Of the present British Museum this beginning forms a very insignificant part. The nucleus was established however; and soon eminent men, who valued their literary and scientific collections as storehouses that should be accessible to all classes of students, began to turn their attention to the collections in Montague House. Foremost among the donors George the Second should be mentioned, as having made over to the nation the royal library, together with the right of demanding a copy of every book entered at Stationers' Hall. Successively, the libraries of Sir Joseph Banks, Dr. Birch, Sir John Hawkins, Dr. Burney and Garrick, and the Royal, Arundel, Lansdowne, Bridgewater, and other MSS. were added to the great store. Captain Cook returned home with additions to the museum of natural history; Sir William Hamilton's collection of vases was purchased in 1772; the spoils of Abercrombie's Egyptian campaign enriched the museum with some fine Egyptian antiquities; grants of money secured the Townley marbles, the Phigalian sculptures, and at last the Elgin marbles; and of late, the accessions to the vast collection, including Layard's treasures, the Xanthian marbles, fossils, birds, curiosities, from the frozen seas, China, the solitudes of Central Africa, and other remote places, where scientific men have been of late prosecuting their studies have been received. In 1823 it was allowed by Parliament that the collection had grown too large for the house in which it was crammed; and accordingly in this year it was resolved to destroy the old residence of the Earl of Halifax, and build a new structure on its site. Sir Robert Smirke, the architect of the present structure, has certainly had good cause to complain of the niggardly supplies voted from time to time for the building, which has been twenty-eight years in progress. The regulations for the admission of the public have fairly kept pace with the progress of those liberal ideas to which the collection is greatly indebted, and of which it is a monument. It will be interesting for the visitor of to-day, to contrast the rules by which he is admitted, with those that fettered his ancestors of the eighteenth century. In the year 1759, the trustees of this institution published their "Statutes and Rules relating to the Inspection and Use of the British Museum." This instructive document may now serve to illustrate the darkness from which, even now, we are struggling. Those visitors who now consider it rather an affront to be required to give up their cane or umbrella at the entrance to our museums and galleries, will be astonished to learn, that in the early days of the museum, those persons who wished to inspect the national collection, were required to make previous application to the porter, in writing, stating their names, condition, and places of abode, as also the day and hour at which they desired to be admitted. Their applications were written down in a register, which was submitted every evening to the librarian or secretary in attendance. If this official, judging from the condition and ostensible character of an applicant, deemed him eligible for admittance, he directed the porter to give him a ticket on the following day. Thus the candidate for admission was compelled to make two visits, before he could learn whether it was the gracious will of a librarian or secretary that he should be allowed the privilege of inspecting Sir Hans Sloane's curiosities. If successful, his trouble did not end when he obtained the ticket; for it was provided by the trustees that no more than ten tickets should be given out for each hour of admittance. Accordingly, every morning on which the museum was accessible, the porter received a company of ten ticket-holders at nine o'clock, ushered them into a waiting-room "till the hour of seeing the museum had come," to quote the words of the trustees. This party was divided into two groups of five persons, one being placed under the direction of the under-librarian, and the other under that of the assistant in each department. Thus attended, the companies traversed the galleries; and, on a signal being given by the tinkling of a bell, they passed from one department of the collection into another:--an hour being the utmost time allowed for the inspection of one department. This system calls to mind the dragooning practised in Westminster Abbey, under the command of the gallant vergers, to the annoyance of leisurely visitors, and of ardent but not active archaeologists. Sometimes, when public curiosity was particularly excited, the number of respectable applicants for admission to the museum exceeded the limit of the prescribed issue. In these cases, tickets were given for remote days; and thus, at times, when the lists were heavy, it must have been impossible for a passing visitor in London to get within the gateway of Montague House. In these old regulations the trustees provided also, that when any person, having obtained tickets, was prevented from making use of them at the appointed time, he was to send them back to the porter, in order "that other persons wanting to see the museum might not be excluded." Three hours was the limit of the time any company might spend in the museum; and those who were so unreasonable or inquisitive as to be desirous of visiting the museum more than once, might apply for tickets a second time "provided that no person had tickets at the same time for more than one." The names of those persons who, in the course of a visit, wilfully transgressed any of the rules laid down by the trustees, were written in a register, and the porter was directed not to issue tickets to them again.

These regulations secured the exclusive attendance of the upper classes. The libraries were hoarded for the particular enjoyment of the worm, whose feast was only at rare intervals disturbed by some student regardless of difficulties. To the poor, worn, unheeded authors of those days, serenely starving in garrets, assuredly the British Museum must have been as impenetrable as a Bastille. We imagine the prim under-librarian glancing with a supercilious expression upon the names and addresses of many poor, aspiring, honourable men--men, whose "condition," to use the phrase of the trustees, bespoke not the gentility of that vulgar age. In those days the weaver and the carpenter would as soon have contemplated a visit to St. James's Palace as have hoped for an admission ticket to the national museum.

These mean precautions of the last century, contrast happily with the enlightened liberty of this. Crowds of all ranks and conditions besiege the doors of the British Museum, especially in holiday times, yet the skeleton of the elephant is spotless, and the bottled rattlesnakes continue to pickle in peace. The Elgin marbles have suffered no abatement of their marvellous beauties; and the coat of the cameleopard is with out a blemish. The Yorkshireman has his unrestrained stare at Sesostris;

the undertaker spends his holiday over the mummies, and no official suppresses his professional objections to the coffins. The weaver observes the looms of the olden time: the soldier compares the Indian's blunt instrument with his own keen and deadly bayonet. The poor needlewoman enjoys her laugh at the rude sewing-instruments of barbarous tribes: the stone-mason perhaps compares his tombs with the sarcophagi of ancient masters. No attendant is deputed to dog the heels of five visitors and to watch them with the cold eye of a gaoler; no bell warns the company from one spot to another: all is open--free!

Through the bright new galleries of Sir Robert Smirke, crowded with the natural productions of every clime, the printed thoughts of the greatest and best men, the marvellous art of forgotten ages, and the poor barbarisms of savage life, we propose to conduct the visitor, in

FOUR DISTINCT VISITS.

VISIT THE FIRST.

On arriving in front of the British Museum for the first time, the visitor will not fail to notice the Grecian Ionic facade, ornamented with forty-four columns, and rising at its extreme point to the height of sixty-six feet. The sculpture which decorates the tympanum of the portico is the work of Sir Richard Westmacott, and is an allegorical representation of the progress of civilisation. The spiritual influences that have successively worked upon the savage natures of the dark ages, have here distinct types. Religion tames the savage; Paganism makes him a crouching sensualist; the Egyptian sees a God in the stars of heaven; and then the mathematician, the musician, the poet, and the painter set to work, and these prophets of mysterious beauties realise civilised mankind. The visitor enters the museum, after ascending a noble flight of steps, by a massive carved oak door, into a fine entrance hall, the ceiling of which is highly coloured, and the general decoration of which is Grecian Ionic. Here he will observe, in addition to one or two of the Nineveh sculptures, at once, three statues: one of the aristocratic lady sculptor, the Honourable Mrs. Damer; Chantrey's statue of Sir Joseph Banks; and Roubillac's study of Shakspeare, presented to the museum by David Garrick. Before entering the galleries of the museum the visitor should observe, that the building faces the four points of the compass, and that the facade forms the southern line. This observation will facilitate a careful and regular examination of the interior. Branching westward from the entrance hall, then eastward to the gallery, is a noble flight of seventy steps, the walls of the staircase being richly inlaid with marble. Having ascended this staircase, the visitor's attention is at once arrested by two stuffed giraffes--the giraffe of North Africa, and the giraffe of South Africa, given to the museum by the late Earl of Derby. These striking zoological specimens at once introduce the visitor to

THE SOUTHERN (CENTRAL) ZOOLOGICAL ROOM,

which is devoted, together with the next room to the east, to Hoofed Animals. Looking eastward from the western side of the room he will observe at once that his way lies down a passage, marked on either side by formidable zoological specimens, which he would rather meet, with their present anatomy of hay, than in their natural condition. In the first room, near the giraffes, stand the walrus of the North Sea; the African rhinoceros; and the Manilla buffalo. He will next observe, that the walls of the room are lined with glass cases, about twelve feet in height, and that in these cases various stuffed animals are grouped. The groups in this room include the varieties of the Antelope, Sheep, and Goats. Grouped together in two or three cases, are the sable and other antelopes from the Cape of Good Hope; the algazelle, and the addax and its young from North Africa; the sing-sing, and the koba from Western Africa; the sassaybi; the chamois of the Alps--the subject of many a stirring mountain song; the goats of North Africa; the strange Siberian ibex; the grue and gorgon from the Cape; varieties of the domestic goat, and the beautiful Cashmere goat. Here also are specimens of sheep, including the wild sheep from the Altai; the bearded sheep of North Africa; the American arguli; the nahorr and caprine antelopes from Nepal; and upon the higher shelves of the cases are grouped the gazelles from Senegal, Nepal, and Madras, whose praises have been sung more than once. The beauty and grace of these delicate creatures, with their taper active limbs, and the soft expression of their heads, may be faintly gathered even from these inanimate stuffed skins with the glassy eyes instead of "the soft blue" celebrated by the poet. Grouped hereabouts are also the four-horned antelope of India; the pigmy antelope from the coast of Guinea; and the madoka from Abyssinia. Before leaving this room, or ante-room, to the great zoological sections of the museum, the visitor should notice the varieties of horns,--straight and tortuous, but all graceful,--of different kinds of hoofed animals.

Advancing eastward the visitor arrives in

THE SOUTHERN ZOOLOGICAL GALLERY.

Here the visitor is still in the midst of the hoofed beasts. The way lies between two rows of animals. Of these the visitor should notice particularly the wild oxen of India and Java; compare the Indian rhinoceros with that of South Africa; and notice the hippopotamus family, from South Africa, as well as a diminutive specimen of the Indian elephant, and a half-grown elephant, from Africa. Having noticed these ponderous creatures, the attention of the visitor will be next attracted to the Llamas, which are arranged in the first two wall-cases. Of these, the wild are generally brown, and the tame of mixed colours. The next fourteen wall-cases are filled with specimens of the different species of Oxen and the Elephant tribe. Among the former the visitor should notice the white bulls of Scotland and Poland: the splendid Lithuanian bison, with his shaggy throat, a present from the Russian Emperor; the bison of the American prairies; and the elando. The specimens of the elephant tribe, ranged in the upper compartments of these cases, include the tapir of South America; the tennu, from Sumatra; the European boar, with its young; the Brazilian peccari: and other curious animals. Here, too, are specimens of the Armadillo tribe. The attention of the visitor will, however, be soon riveted upon an animal which, with the beak of a duck and the claws of a bird, has the body of an otter. In Australia (its native country) this singular animal is commonly called a water mole, but to scientific men it is known as the mullingong; it is placed in the same order with its neighbour, the spring-ant or echidra, also a native of Australia. Before leaving these cases, the visitor should pause to notice the Sloths, and particularly the repulsive aspect of the yellow-faced sloth of South America.

The visitor should now pass to the cases marked from 17 to 30. These are devoted to the Horse tribe and Deer. Here the reindeer from Hudson's Bay, the red fallow deer of Europe, the elk, and the cheetul of India, will catch the eye immediately. The beautiful South African zebra is here also, grouped near the Asiatic wild ass, and the Zoological Society's hybrids of the zebra, wild ass, and common donkey. The upper shelves of the cases are devoted, as usual, to the smaller specimens of the tribe below. Here are the European roebuck, the West African water musk, the Javan musk, the white-bellied and golden-eyed musk. Having examined these zoological specimens, the visitor should proceed on his way east to

THE MAMMALIA SALOON.

This saloon is one of the most interesting parts of the exhibition to the general visitor, as he sees here at a glance the various classes of the highest order of the animal creation, all grouped after their kinds, and in that gradation of development which nature has assigned them. Those specimens which are placed on the floor in the central space of the room include some large varieties of the Bears, and a few small specimens of Seals, including the young of the harp seal, with the white fur, which clothes them on their first appearance in the world, and the young of the Cape of Good Hope eared seal; but these isolated specimens should not engage the attention of the visitor before he has followed the systematic arrangement or classification adopted with regard to the animals deposited in the wall-cases that line the saloon. The first series or family of animals to which, according to Cuvier, his particular attention should be attracted are

THE MONKEYS,

ranged in the first eleven wall-cases. These cases contain the species of monkeys found in the Old World. The varieties in colour, shape, size, and attitude, are endless. Here are the green monkeys from Western Africa; the white-throated monkey from India; the bearded monkey, with a republican air about him; and the monkey who appears to have had his ears pulled, but is in reality known to scientific men as the red-eared monkey; both from Fernando Po: the Risley of monkeys, called the vaulting monkey, with his white nose; and the talapoin, from Western Africa; the gaudy macaque, known as the brilliant from Japan; that dingy gentleman, the sooty mangabey, from Africa: the African chimpanzee (to whom satirical gentlemen with a turn for zoological comparisons, are greatly indebted); the ourang-outan, with his young, from Borneo; the presbytes, dusky and starred, from Singapore, Malacca, and Borneo; and the drill and mandrill, from Africa. The Monkeys of the New World are grouped in six cases (12-18). Herein the visitor should particularly notice the curious spider monkeys, from Brazil and Bolivia: the negro monkey; the apes, with large eyes, like those of the owl, called night apes; the howlers, so called from the incessant howling they maintain at night in their native forests; the quaint marmozettes and handsome silky monkeys; and the Jew monkeys. The next two cases contain specimens of the lemurs, more familiarly known as Madagascar monkies. Of these the flying lemur is the most remarkable species. Specimens of this species are grouped in the lower part of the cases; they are from the Indian Archipelago; and in the texture of their skin and the loose and light way in which it connects their limbs, they resemble bats. They nurse their young by forming a kind of couch with their body suspended downwards from the branches of a tree.

It now remains for the visitor to direct his attention to the fine collection of
RAPACIOUS ANIMALS,
ranged in thirty-two distinct wall-cases in this room. The first tribe, taking the cases in their order of succession, to which the visitor's attention will be attracted on passing from the cases of lemurs, is
THE CAT TRIBE.

The animals which he will find grouped in the first seven cases (21-27) are properly Cats. Here is the South African lion, the fine black leopard, which is pointed out to visitors as a beast that killed its keeper; the lynxes of Spain, Sardinia, and America; the wild cats of Europe; the curious booted-cat, imported from the Cape of Good Hope; the American ocelots; and the Asiatic and African chaus. These animals are picturesquely grouped in seven cases. In the next case, in order of succession (28), are the hyaenas of South Africa and Egypt. Here are the spotted hyaena, with its young; and the striped hyaena. The three following cases are filled with varieties of the civet family (esteemed for the strong scent which some of them, as the African cibet and the Chinese and Indian zibet, yield), including the hyaena civet from the Cape of Good Hope: genets and ichneumons, which will be found on the lower shelves; and the Mexican house-marten. The five following cases are filled with the varieties of
THE DOG FAMILY.

Here the sporting visitor may amuse himself by examining the points of the Dogs of the four quarters of the globe. Here are the well-known Newfoundland dog, the wild dogs of different climates, the four-toed hunting dog of Abyssinia and South Africa, the Cape of Good Hope dog, with its long ears; the varieties of fox and wolf; all expressing great activity and extraordinary cunning. Ladies will be pleased to notice a lap-dog almost hidden by his long hair, placed under a particular glass-case: this exclusive little aristocrat is from Mexico.

In the next case to which the visitor will direct his attention (38) are grouped the varieties of the Mustelina, or Martens, of America and Europe. These lesser specimens of the cat tribe, include the weasels of Himalaya, Mexico, and Siberia; the American and European polecats: the lesser otters, from the north of America and Europe; and the curious animal known as the false sable of America. It is amusing to notice the sameness of expression--that of cunning--shown in the heads of every specimen of the cat tribe. The next case (39) introduces the visitor to those mammalia which are included in

THE BEAR TRIBE.

This tribe includes the Racoons, Otters, Badgers, Skunks, Gluttons, and Bears. The case to which the visitor's attention is now directed, contains the varieties of the glutton family--the Chinese musk weasel; the European and North American badgers; the Javan stinkard, and the American skunks and conepats.

The next case (40) is devoted to the otter family. These ingenious animals are found in the four quarters of the world. Here are the common European otter; the otters of Java and India; the clawless African otter, from the Cape of Good Hope; and the sea and muffled otters, from America. Next to these interesting animals, are some of the bears, including the savage Arctic white bear, the Malay bear, and the Indian sloth bear. Next to these bears, the racoons are grouped, and they close the collection illustrative of the bear tribe. In the case following those which contain the racoons is one (43) in which the varieties of

THE MOLE TRIBE

are arranged. These include Moles from the four quarters of the world. There are the North American marsh moles and long-tailed star-nosed moles; the golden moles, from the Cape of Good Hope; the varieties of the shrew-mouse, including the remarkable blue shrew-mouse of India, the African elephant shrew, and the Russian musk shrew; the Javan insectivorous squirrel; and a curious variety of hedgehogs, from opposite quarters of the globe. Having examined these inferior mammalia, the visitor will pass in direct order of succession to the cases in which

THE MARSUPIAL ANIMALS

are deposited. These fill nine wall-cases, and they should be carefully examined, as exhibiting a peculiar economy of animal life. The marsupial animals are placed by some zoologists in the lowest class of mammalia. They include carnivorous, herbivorous, and insectivorous families, and their head-quarters appear to be Australia. In the first two cases (44, 45) which the visitor will examine, are the varieties of Australian phalangers; and here also are the New Holland bears, the Australian wombat, the flying squirrel of Norfolk Island, the flying phalangers; and in the right corner of the case are grouped those notable animals to which public curiosity has of late years been so keenly directed--the kangaroos. In the next five cases (46-51) the visitor will find more varieties of these strange, awkward-looking creatures. Here amid the kangaroos of Australia are the long-nosed, rock, and jerboa kangaroos, the New Guinea tree-kangaroo, and below, the Australian koala. The two next cases (52, 53) contain the varieties of Australian opossums, and below are the opossums of America.

These close the attractions of the wall-cases, and the visitor should now glance round the saloon at the specimens of the varieties of

THE SEAL TRIBE,

which are arranged along the tops of the wall-cases. These include the leonine seal of the Southern Ocean, the Cape porpoise and dolphin, and the long-beaked dolphin of the Ganges. Having noticed these specimens, the visitor should proceed to examine the extensive collection of

CORALS,

which are arranged upon the central tables of the saloon. To explain the presence of coral in the midst of a zoological collection it is necessary to remind the visitor that this beautiful substance, which is chiefly a deposit of carbonate of lime, is also the fossil remains of that animal known to zoologists as the polypus. These polypi put forth buds, which remain attached to the parental polypus, and generate other buds; and in this way countless polypi, linked together, yet maintaining a separate and distinct existence, spread themselves over miles and miles of submarine rocks, in endless varieties of shape, and leave their remains to be dredged by the hardy fisherman, for the adornment of beauty. These beautiful polypi skeletons cluster in curious formations, as the visitor will perceive on examining the fine collection of corals before him.[1] Among the remarkable coral formations to which the general visitor's attention may be directed, are the sea-mushroom, the remains of a single polypus of great size; the brainstone, which presents a circular mass of long winding cells, and altogether has the appearance of the masses and veins of the brain; the sea-pen, and the sea-fan. In the cases, ranged together in the saloon, the visitor who feels interested in the infinite varieties of coral formation, will find specimens that will give him a full idea of the architectural abilities of the active zoophytes that carry on their operations upon the rocks that lie not far below the surface of the ocean. From the coral tables, the visitor's way lies out of the Mammalia Saloon to the north, into a gallery of which all Englishmen who understand the value of a perfect museum, are justly proud.

THE EASTERN ZOOLOGICAL GALLERY

of the British Museum runs the entire length of the building. It is divided into five compartments, and its space is devoted to the display of Birds, Shells, and a few Paintings. The birds exhibited in this gallery fill no less than one hundred and sixty-six wall-cases; and the shells which are distributed throughout the central space occupy fifty large tables: the lesser tables which are placed here and there near the birds, being devoted to the display of birds' eggs. The pictures are hung above the wall-cases. This general glance at the arrangement of the gallery, will prevent the visitor from falling into the error of distracting his attention from one order of zoological development to another at frequent intervals. Already he has examined the various species of animal life which rank in the highest class--the mammalia. Before him now, are ranged vast numbers of the second class of animal life; and he will do well to pay these some attention, and to get definite impressions regarding them, before he turns to the other attractions which the museum offers. Before proceeding to examine the first order of birds which are in the first eastern room, the visitor should glance at the historical portraits suspended above the cases. Among them he will find a Mary Queen of Scots, by Cornelius Jansen; a Cromwell, presented by the Protector to Colonel Rich of the parliamentary forces, by whose great-grandson it was bequeathed to the trustees of the museum; William Duke of Cumberland by Morier; Zucchero's Queen Elizabeth; Sir Peter Lely's Charles the Second; and the Queen of George the Second by Jarvis. Having sufficiently examined these works, the visitor should at once begin his inspection of the Raptores or

BIRDS OF PREY.

These include some splendid ornithological specimens. They are divided into two families: those who pursue their depredations by day; and those which wait till night cloaks their proceedings. It is almost possible to read the special instincts of the two families in their formation, and expression. The daring expressed in the fierce glances of the eagles and falcons, bespeaks the fearless spoliator, in broad daylight and in the face of an enemy; whereas the large vacant eyes of the owls, have a cruel, coward look, that stamps the midnight assassin.

In the first case the visitor will notice the strongbearded vulture of the Alpine and Himalayan mountains. The next six cases (2-7) are filled with the varieties of the Vulture, including the American, carrion, black, and king vultures; the South African sociable vulture; the angola vulture from Congo; and, towering above all, the great condor of the Andes, with his immense breadth of wing. The vultures, with their fierce and cruel aspect, are, nevertheless, cowardly birds, and feed rather upon dead bodies than venture to kill for themselves.

Next in order, after the vultures, the visitor will find the Eagle branch of the falcon family distributed in ten cases (8-17). This family includes some handsome birds. Foremost amongst these the visitor will remark the athletic golden eagle of Europe, a frequenter of Great Britain. This bird preys upon hares and rabbits, and has been known to plant its claws in a young lamb with success. In this vicinity are also the Indian Pondicherry eagle, sacred to the Brahmins; the Egyptian booted eagle; the Brazilian eagle; the South American harpy eagle; the European Jean le Blanc eagle; the marine eagle of the Indian Archipelago; the South American crested goshawk; the varieties of the osprey; and the short-tailed falcon from the Cape of Good Hope. Next after the eagles, are ranged the Kites and Buzzards (18-24). These include the South American caracaras; the European rough-legged falcon; the European kite; the Indian colny falcon; varieties of the honey buzzard; and the North American spotted-tailed hobby. The true falcons follow next in order of succession (24-26). The courage of these birds is familiar to all who have read of the hunting days of old. In the cases before the visitor, are grouped the European hobby and kestrel, and the peregrine and jet falcons. Many visitors from the country will be familiar with some of the sparrow-hawks in the next case (27). They may be often seen sweeping swiftly along near the earth, intent upon their prey. The last cases of diurnal birds of prey (28-30) contain the Harriers. These are birds of prey that meet their victims on the ground, and frequent bog-lands. The specimens here presented, include the secretary of the Cape of Good Hope; the chanting falcon from the same region; the ash-coloured falcon, hen-harrier, and Madagascar falcon.

And now, proceeding on his easterly way, the visitor approaches the Birds that Prey by Night. They are solemnly assembled in five cases. Their reputed wisdom has its parallel in the human family: we also have our owls, with their large eyes and solemn demeanour, who cheat people into the idea that there must be something in all that solemnity and gravity of expression. Poets of the dismal school, however, owe a great debt of gratitude to these mysterious and unsociable birds. The visitor will at once call to mind the usual sequel of poems that open with the hooting of the owl, or with the intimation that it is the hour when the wise bird opens his eyes with some effect. Let us glance at the varieties of the dismal family before which we have brought the visitor. Here are the snowy owl of North America and the hawk owls. In the cases (32, 33) are grouped the eagle owls, including the great-eared owls, and the North American Virginian eared owl. The next two cases contain the howlets, including the Tengmalm's owl of the north of Europe; the Javan bay owl, and the barn white owls of various countries. These birds close the collection of birds of prey; and the visitor, refraining from the temptation to inspect the central tables, for the present, should advance into the room, the wall-cases of which are filled with

PERCHING BIRDS.

The perching birds are subdivided into five families: the Wide-gaping; the Slender-Beaked; the Toothed-Beaked; the Cone-Beaked; and the Climbers, or Scansores. The family of wide-gaping birds, is that ranged first in order, occupying cases 36 to 42. The visitor will first remark the goatsuckers with their wide bills and large eyes, adapted to catch the insects on which they feed. The varieties here collected, include the great goatsucker; the goatsuckers of Europe, New Holland, North America, and Africa; and the wedge-tailed goatsucker. The next case (38) contains specimens of the varieties of Swallows and Swifts, including those of North America; the esculent swallow of the Indian Archipelago; and the sandmartin of Europe. In the two following cases (39, 40) are grouped the varieties of the tody and broadbills, from the West Indies, and Brazil; and the curncuis from the southern parts of Asia and America. The visitor next arrives before two cases (41, 42) of birds of brilliant plumage, suggestive of the regions where the humming birds float in the air "like winged flowers." The kingfisher at times startles the English pedestrian when he is sauntering near a high-banked brook;--its gaudy plumage contrasts so forcibly with the sober tints of our English song birds, that he is at first inclined to take the gay fellow for a truant cage bird. But the fisher is quite at home, and is probably diving for his fish dinner. The kingfishers grouped in the two cases before which the visitor now stands, include specimens of the Australian brown kingfisher; the green and great jacamars of South America; the European bee eater; the Javan night bird;

and the Ternate kingfisher from the Philippine Islands. Having feasted his eyes upon the gaudy colours of these feathered fishermen, the visitor will find in the next case (43) the first specimens of the slender-beaked perching birds. These slender beaks are divided into sub-families of Sun Birds; Humming Birds; Honey Eaters; and the Creepers, &c. The sun birds live upon the pollen of flowers. The specimens here grouped together, include the numerous species of African and South American sun birds; the paradise birds of Molucca; the promerops of New Guinea and Africa; the Sandwich Islands honey eater; and the Australian rifle bird. Next in order are grouped the famous American humming birds (44). These brilliant little creatures, not larger than moths, are famed for their beauty all over the world. The delicacy of their structure, the splendour of the colours in which they are habited, their poetical diet, and the impossibility of keeping them alive in a confined state, are the attributes of delicacy and beauty which have made them objects of interest to all persons who have any insight to the mysterious graces of animal organisation. So brilliant is the plumage of some of the varieties, that they have been named after gems: thus, in the case before which the visitor has arrived, he will find the garnet-throated humming bird, and the topaz humming bird. Next to these brilliant creatures of the south, in case **45** are the curious Australian honey eaters, with their feathered tongues, made to brush the sweet essences from flowers: and the two following cases contain the remaining varieties of the slender-beaked family. Here are the Creepers of Europe; the Nuthatches of North America and Europe; varieties of the Wren; and the Warblers of Guiana and Patagonia. The visitor next approaches the varieties of the family known as the tooth-beaked perching birds. To this family our choicest songsters belong. They fill five cases (48-52). The visitor will observe in the first of the four cases, the tailor birds, remarkable for the fantastic domes they form to their nests; the Australian superb warbler; and the Dartford warbler of Europe. The common song birds of Europe are grouped here, including blackcaps, wrens, the active little titmice, together with the North American wood warblers. Next to these are cases (53-55) of Thrushes, including the tropical ant thrushes; the Javan mountain warbler; the Brazilian king thrush; the rock thrushes: the imitative Australian thrush; the blackbird; the North American mimic thrush; the Chinese and South American thrushes, celebrated for their babbling; the yellow orioles, of Europe and the east; and here also are the short-legged thrushes of the tropics.

The two next cases (56, 57) contain the Flycatchers, which catch insects on the wing. The varieties to be seen here include the South American pikas and shrikes, with their gay plumage. These shrikes[2]--better known as butcher-birds--are so called from the cruelty with which they treat their prey. In the second case of flycatchers are grouped the true flycatchers, which are mostly from the old world; those from America being the solitary flycatcher, the black-headed flycatcher, the king and broad-billed tody, and the white-eared thrush. In the two next cases (58, 59) are the families of the Chatterers, with their resplendent plumage. In the first case, are groups of the Asiatic and American thick-heads, and the gorgeous little Manakins of South America and Australia. They are called after their colours, as the speckled manakin, the white-capped South American manakin, the purple-breasted, variegated, purple-throated, and rock manakins. Next to the manakins, are the Indian, African, and American caterpillar eaters; the Malabar and African shrikes; and in the two last cases of the tooth-beaked group, are placed the true butcher-birds and bush shrikes.

The next group of perching birds are the cone-beaked. This group includes the large family of the Crows to which the birds of paradise of New Guinea are allied; that of the Finches, with their relations from every clime; and the Hornbills, remarkable for the size and strength of their bills. The first two cases (62, 63) devoted to this group, contain the varieties of the Crow family. Here the visitor should notice the finely-marked jays from various parts of the world; the noisy and piping rollers of Australia and New Guinea; the crows, rooks, and jackdaws from various parts of Europe; the New Zealand wattle bird; the African changeable crow; and the rufous crow of India. The next case (64) is bright with the gleaming plumage of the New Guinea crows, or birds of paradise; and here, too, are the curious grakles--the foetid and the bare-necked from South America; and the Alpine and red-legged crows, or choughs, of elevated lands. Next in succession is a case (65) in which are grouped the shining thrushes of Australia, Asia, and Africa, which include the ingenious and tasteful satin bower birds, that form decorated bowers of twigs and shells to sport in; and here amid the grakles of the Indian Archipelago will be found those curious birds, that gather their sustenance from insect larvas which secrete in the coarse skin of the rhinoceros: these birds are known under the name of African beef-eaters. The Starlings, which are also of the crow family, are grouped in the case

(66) next to that in which the visitor found the beef-eaters and shining thrushes. They resemble the beef-eaters closely in their mode of life, like them deriving their food from the insect life that congregates upon various kinds of cattle. Starlings are found in all the quarters of the globe, and present many varieties, as the observer of the case under notice will see. Here are the rose-coloured thrushes of Europe; the grakles of Malabar, India, South Africa, and South America; and the stares of America and Europe. The next case contains the varieties of the American Icteric Orioles, which lay their eggs in the nests of other birds, like the cuckoo. Among the varieties, the visitor should notice the red-winged, crested, and banana orioles. The African and Indian Weavers, so called from the peculiar construction of their nests, occupy the case (68) next to that filled by the orioles. Here are also the African, European, and American grosbeaks, so christened from that strength of bill which enables them to demolish hard fruits. Among these are the African widow birds; the Galapagos ground sparrows. The beauty of the Tanagers of North and South America is well known. In order of succession they here follow the grosbeaks (68, 69), and present a brilliant group, including the golden tanager, the red-breasted, the summer, and the bishop. And then the Finches, in all their varieties of colour and size, occupy two cases (69, 70). Here, among the more sober and unassuming of the numerous family, the visitor will notice the common sparrow that chirps cheerfully through the smoke of London alleys; the brown linnet with its lively notes; the gayer goldfinches, greenfinches, chaffinches, the North American songfinch, and the many varieties of the buntings, including the epicure's ortolans that are found in various parts of the world. Next in order to the finches, the Larks are grouped in a single case (71) with other varieties of the great finch family. These birds sing as they soar into the air; and on cloudless days, how often do the happy notes of the skylark come down to the wanderer upon earth, with a cheerful influence:--

"... The lark that sings in heaven
Builds its nest upon the ground."

Here, with the larks, are several curious birds, including the crossbeaks of Europe, the grosbeak of the South Sea Islands, the plant cutters of South America, and the colies of India and the Cape, that sleep in companies each suspended by one foot. The two last cases of the cone-beaked perching birds, are devoted to those birds known collectively as Hornbills, from the size and formation of their bills. These remarkable birds are said to be another off-shoot of "the great corvine nest;" and the author of "The Vestiges of Creation" regards the hollow protuberance upon the upper mandible (which is the distinguishing feature of the family), as "a sounding-board to increase the vociferation which these birds delight to utter." The remarkable varieties in the cases, are the helmet hornbill of India, and the African rhinoceros hornbill. These birds prey upon small birds and reptiles, which they toss into the air and then swallow whole.

The Scansores, or Climbers, form the last section of the perching birds. This is an interesting group, since it includes all the varieties of the parrot, cockatoo, and macaw species; the woodpeckers, the toucans, and the cuckoos.

The visitor will arrive first before the three cases (74-76) devoted to the Parrots, Cockatoos, and Macaws. The gaudy colours which they display, and their well-known habits and powers, always ensure them a large circle of spectators. Here the visitor should notice the red-crowned parrot, and ground parrot of Australia; the South American yellow-headed, and hawk-headed parrots; the horned parrot from New Caledonia and the racket-tailed parrot of the Philippines. Among the Macaws are the hyacinthine macaw of South America, and the blue and yellow varieties. Among the Cockatoos, the visitor should notice the great white cockatoo from the Indian Archipelago; and here also are the Alexandrine parroquet and the Papuan lory. The Toucans, which inhabit the deep recesses of tropical American forests, here occupy the next case (77). They are recognised as a branch of the great corvine family. Their enormous beaks are peculiarly adapted for searching in quest of eggs about the crevices of trees. The varieties here, include the Janeiro toucan, and the yellow-breasted toucan. The three next cases contain the many varieties of the Woodpecker. Woodpeckers are represented by naturalists as crows with a structure adapted to "an insect-eating life amidst growing timber." They are to be found in all quarters of the globe, searching out, with their long beaks, the minute life that gathers in the interstices of trees. The first case of the series, contains the South American and African barbets, and the groove-billed barbican; the minute woodpecker, the North American three-toed and white-billed woodpecker, and the spotted woodpecker common in Europe. In the second case are the larger varieties of the woodpecker, including the well-known great black woodpecker of Europe; the North American red-headed woodpecker, and the South American yellow-crested variety; the Carolina woodpecker; and the Cayenne woodpecker. The third case contains the African and American ground woodpeckers; and the Wrynecks of Africa, Europe, and India. The chief food of the wrynecks consists of ants, which they pick up with their delicately tapered tongues.

The three last cases devoted to perching birds, are occupied by the varieties of the Cuckoo family. In this country, the notes of the cuckoo are hailed as the announcement of the dawning summer; and the solitary and peculiar habits of the bird, but particularly its custom of placing its eggs in the nests of larks, finches, sparrows, &c., and so getting alien birds to bring up its young, have always made it an object of particular curiosity to people generally. This latter custom has been explained, by a high authority, thus:--"The fact is, that the cuckoo is obliged by its constitutional character to stay an unusually short time in the northern regions where it produces its young. In our country its normal stay is only from the middle of April to the beginning of July. Belated in its approach to the nursing regions, it is obliged to make use of the nests of other birds, which it finds ready built. What is worthy of notice, it employs the nests of its own nearest relations, the larks, pipits, finches, sparrows, &c.--an arrangement we may suppose to be connected in some way with the early history of the whole group of species--a family or clan sacrifice, as it were, for the benefit of a less fortunate member."[3] In the first case of cuckoos, are the African honey cuckoos, and the South American rain cuckoos. The birds of the former of these varieties are noted for guiding depredators to the wild honeycombs; and the latter live upon insects, snakes, and fruits. Here too are the Coucals of Africa, Java, South America, and Australia, including the Australian giant coucal, the Asiatic, South American, and West Indian anis; and the two cuckoos of the tropics, including the gilded cuckoo, the greatspotted cuckoo, and white-crested cuckoo from Africa, and the common European cuckoo. Before leaving the region devoted to perching birds, the visitor should glance at a few of the pictures which are suspended above the cases in this compartment. They include, amongst various portraits of British Museum donors, three of Sir Hans Sloane, one by Murray; Robert Earl of Oxford, by Sir Godfrey Kneller; and Edward Earl of Oxford, by Dahl.

The visitor's way now lies to the north, into the third, or central compartment

of the gallery, the wall cases of which contain the gallinaceous, or
SCRAPING BIRDS.

This order is divided into four distinct families--the Pigeons, the Curassows, the Pheasants, and the Grouse and Partridge tribe. Of these families the museum contains a fine and complete collection. The beauty of the pheasant family--its varieties ranging from the gaudy splendour of the peacock to the more modest beauty of the common hen--are here fully represented.

In the first case (84) of Scraping Birds, are grouped the Asiatic, African, and Australian tree pigeons, which inhabit the woods, and live on berries and various kinds of seeds. The collection includes the Javan black-capped pigeon, and the parrot and aromatic pigeons of India. The two next cases (85, 86) are filled with the true pigeons and turtles of various parts of the world, in all their varieties--the Indian nutmeg pigeon, and the Australian antarctic pigeon. The next case is devoted to the common European turtle and the North American migratory pigeon. The next case is filled with the varieties of the ground Dove, among which the visitor should notice the ground turtle, the West Indian partridge pigeon, the great crowned pigeon of the Indian Isles, and the bronze-winged pigeon of Australia. Leaving the pigeons behind, the visitor's attention is next called to the two cases of Curassows (89, 90), the poultry peculiar to South America. They feed on fruit, worms, and insects; and live in small flocks. The curassows are followed by the varieties of the pheasant tribe, grouped in thirteen cases (91-103). The three first cases are given up to the splendid East Indian Pheasants known to Europeans generally, as peacocks. They were brought to the west and valued for the beauty of their plumage many centuries before the Christian era, and no doubt helped to inflame the imagination of the Mediterranean merchants who dreamt of the untold wealth of the Indies. The specimens of these birds here preserved, are fine samples of the species. They include the iris and crested peacocks, the Japan peacock, the Thibet crossoptilon, and the Argus pheasant. The two following cases (94, 95) of the pheasant family contain the varieties of true Asiatic pheasants; but the visitor's attention will be immediately riveted upon the specimens of the splendid Chinese pheasant known as Reeves' Chinese pheasant. The plumage of this pheasant is very beautiful, the feathers of the tail measuring sometimes between five and six feet in length. The three following cases (96-98) are filled with varieties of the pheasant from Indian climes. In the first case are the pheasants from the Himalayan Mountains, and the pencilled variety from China. In the third case the visitor should notice the handsome fire-backed pheasant of Sumatra, the superb pheasant, Sonnerat's wild cock, and the cock of Java. The two following cases (99, 100) contain the remainder of the pheasant varieties. Amongst these the visitor will find, the horned and black-headed pheasants of India, the American turkey, the pintados of Africa and Guinea, and the pheasants from the north of Asia that live upon bulbous roots, known as the Impeyan pheasants. The immediate successors of the pheasants, in point of order, are the Partridges, of which the collection contains three cases (101-103). These birds inhabit both hemispheres, and specimens of the different varieties are grouped in the cases. In the first case the visitor should notice the Currie partridge, from Nepal, the Cape and bare-necked partridges of Africa, and the sanguine pheasant; in the second case, the common European partridge and quail, the red European partridge, the Indian olive partridge, and the Andalusian quail; in the third and last partridge case, Californian and crested quails, and the Indian crowned partridge. Next in order are the Grouse, grouped in two cases (104, 105). In the first of these cases the visitor will notice the wood grouse of Scotland, and the ruffed and other grouse of America; in the second case, the sand-grouse of the scorching deserts. The last case of the scraping birds is occupied by the Sheathbills, which, as the visitor will perceive, closely resemble grouse. They are from South America; the tinamous, from the warmer parts of the Continent; and the megapodius, of Australia and the Asiatic islands.

It now remains for the visitor to notice a few of the paintings suspended in this compartment, above the wall cases. These paintings include a copy of Klingstad's portrait of Peter I. of Russia, three historical portraits, presented to the museum by the Rev. A. Planta, and a hunting scene by Geo. B. Weenix.

The visitor should now advance into the fourth compartment of the gallery, the wall-cases of which are devoted to the specimens of

WADING BIRDS.

Most interesting families of birds are included in this order. First, there are the Ostriches, which are the envy of all people cursed with weak digestive powers; then there is the Dodo, with its mysterious and half-told history; also the Bustards, the Coursers, the Plovers, the Cranes, the Storks, the Sandpipers, the Snipes, &c. These varieties of wading birds are carefully classed, and represented in the compartment of the gallery to which the visitor has now worked his way. First in the order of arrangement stand the ostriches, occupying the cases (107, 109). Some naturalists refuse to class ostriches with the order of wading birds, and elevate them to the dignity of a distinct order, Cursores, or runners; but in the museum, as the visitor will perceive, they are at the head of the wading order. Unscientific people know more about the ostrich than about most other birds of foreign climes. Few people have not heard that the egg of the ostrich weighs three pounds--that the sun is the bird's Cantelo--that he has only two toes to each foot--that he sometimes exceeds six feet in height--and that it would not be an act of madness to back a stout specimen, for speed, against an average horse. The digestion of the ostrich has been considerably strengthened in the minds of unscientific persons by imaginative travellers; the fact being that these birds live upon vegetable food, occasionally swallowing stones, or a bit of iron, in aid of that digestion which has been so misrepresented. In the cases before the visitor are the African ostrich, and his relations, the Australian cassowary, and the American emu--all characterised by the absence of a hind toe. Having noticed these fine birds, the visitor will be anxious to learn something of the mysterious case (108), which contains a foot, the cast of a skull, and a painting. Here he sees all that has yet been traced of the extinct dodo, a bird which is believed to have existed in vast numbers up to a recent period, chiefly on the Bourbon and Mauritius islands. The painting is said to be an authentic Dutch performance, taken from the living bird at the time when the Cape of Good Hope was doubled by adventurous men heated with exaggerated notions of the exhaustless wealth of the Indies. Its precise position among birds has not been finally assigned. It appears to have been incapable of flight, to have had a vulture's head, and the foot of a common fowl. It is conjectured that the race was extinguished by the rapacity of the first settlers in the Mauritius, who, finding the dodo excellent eating and an easy prey, demolished every specimen of the species. Near these wrecks of the dodo, and in the same case, is the New Zealand wingless bird, now almost extinct, but to scientific men an interesting link between the bird and the mammalia. The Bustards occupy the two next cases (110, 111) to which the visitor should direct his attention. Here are the two bustards of the eastern hemisphere, the great European bustard, the African ruffed and white-eared bustards, and the Arabian bustard. The next case (112) contains the varieties of wading birds called, from their power of running, Coursers. These are chiefly found in Africa; but the varieties in the case include, in addition to the North African cream-coloured courser, and the double-collared courser, the thick-kneed European bustard. The Plovers are arranged next in order to the coursers. The varieties included in the case (113) are from Africa, North America, and Europe. Here are, amongst others, the beautiful golden-ringed and dotterel plovers of Europe, and the American noisy plover. In the case which next claims attention (114) are the turnstones, that turn stones on the sea-shore in search of food; the oyster catchers, that wrench shell fish from their shells; and the South American gold-breasted and other trumpeters. The Cranes, of which there is an extensive collection, now claim the visitor's attention. They are from all parts of the world, and love the borders of rivers and lakes, where they can prey upon small reptiles and fish. In the first cases (115-118) are the true cranes, including the common European variety, the Indian crane, the South American caurale snipe, the common and purple-crested herons of Europe, the Pacific heron, the crowned heron, the North American great heron, and the African demoiselle heron. In the two following cases (120, 121) the visitor will find the American blue heron, and the great and little egrets; and in the next two cases given to the crane family (122, 123) are the bittern and little bittern of Europe, the American lineated bittern, the squacco and night herons of Europe, the American night heron, the European spoonbill, and the South American cinereous boatbill. The examination of these varieties will give the visitor a clear idea of the peculiarities of birds that frequent marshes and the borders of streams.

The next case to which the visitor will direct his steps, is that (124) in which the Storks of Europe and America, including the white and black varieties, are grouped. In the case next in order of succession to that given to the storks (125) are some interesting branches of the crane family, including the Indian gigantic crane. Here also are the jabirus of America and Senegal, and the North-American ibis, which will introduce the spectator to the case of ibises, among which is the sacred ibis of the Egyptians; the black-headed Indian ibis; and that of New Holland. Next, in order (127), are the Godwits, which follow the mild seasons from one country to another; among them are the English red godwit; and the Australian terek snipe. In the next case (128) the visitor should examine the varieties of Snipes and

Sand-pipers it contains. These birds hunt their food in gravel and amid stones in most localities. The most remarkable of the group are the lanky avocets, with their long legs adapted to hunt rivers for fish spawn and water insects: among them, the long-legged plover should be noticed. The varieties of the sand-piper, in the next case (129), now claim a careful inspection. Sand-pipers inhabit various parts of the world, and, like the ibises, love the neighbourhood of water, where they seek the food congenial to them. The Phalaropes, which are also represented in this case, are natives of the eternal ice of the arctic regions, where they subsist upon crustacea. The visitor passes from the sand-pipers to the case of Snipes (130), including the British varieties, and the snipe of India. In the next case (131) the visitor should notice the Chinese and South American jacanas, that walk about unconcernedly upon the floating leaves of water plants; with these are grouped the South American Screamers. The three last cases devoted to wading birds, contain the varieties of the British and North American Rails: the varieties of the Gallinule, including the European purple gallinule, the South American variety, and the Australian black-backed variety; and the Finfoots of Africa and America. All these birds inhabit marshy land, or the banks of streams, and derive their food from the insect life that swarms near the water. With the finfoots the collection of wading birds closes; but before going on his way, the visitor should glance at the paintings which are hung about the wall cases in this room or compartment. These include portraits of Lord Chancellor Bacon; Andrew Marvel; a copy from the picture at Wimpole of Admiral Lord Anson; Camden; Matthew Prior; William Cecil, Lord Burghley; Sir Isaac Newton; Archbishop Cranmer; and George Buchanan. Having examined these works, the visitor's way lies in a direct line to the last room of the eastern gallery--to that, the wall cases of which, are filled with the families of

WEB FOOTED BIRDS.

This section of the birds includes all those which are able to support themselves upon the surface of the water. The varieties include the gaudy Flamingos; the Albatross that frighted the ancient mariner; the Pelicans with their pouches; the impetuous Gannets, and the remarkable Frigate Bird. And here, too, the visitor will find the varieties of ducks, geese, and swans, all classed in regular order. The web-footed birds occupy no less than thirty-one cases; to each of which the visitor should pay some attention. The first case of the series (135) is gay with the bright red plumage of the flamingos, with their crooked upper mandible, and their long legs and necks. The next four cases (136-139) of the series are occupied by the varieties of the Goose. In the first of these cases the visitor should notice the varieties of the spur-winged goose from various parts of the world; including the black-backed goose. In the three following cases the white fronted and grey-legged European geese; the Canada and Magellanic geese; and the Indian barred-headed goose; and the cereopsis from New Holland. The stately Swans from various parts of the world, all graceful; including the handsome black-necked swan, and the whistling swan, occupy the three cases next in succession (140-142). The Ducks occupy no less than eight cases; and the visitor will linger over the beautiful varieties, without once allowing the unkind association of green peas to enter his head. In the first four cases (143-146) are the sub-families of the true duck, collected from various parts of the world;--the teal from China; the whistling duck from South America, and the European varieties of the common teal, the widgeon, and the sheldrake. Three cases (147-149) are filled with those sub-families of the duck which prefer the sea or the great lakes, including the handsome red-crested European duck; the eider duck, which is robbed of its down for the comfort of mankind;[4] the scoter and nyroca ducks; and, in the third case, the spinous-tailed ducks of southern climes. The arctic birds, known as the Mergansers, are grouped in the next case (150): and, proceeding on his way, the visitor will arrive before the cases (151-152) of Divers, from the north, so called from the strength with which they dive for the fish upon which they live; but their powers in this respect are not equalled by those of a sub-family of web-footed birds, which the visitor will presently reach. Before reaching the cases in which the interesting sub-families of the Gulls are exhibited the visitor should remark the varieties of the Grebes in case 152; the two following cases devoted to the Auks from the arctic regions; and the true Auks of Britain; the varieties of the Penguins, or marine parrots; and the Guillemots. From these birds the visitor's way lies in the direction of the six cases (155-160) in which the sub-families of the gulls are grouped. The contents of the first cases will at once strike him: here are the Petrels, and the associations of shipwreck and disaster with which they have ever been connected. The group includes the stormy petrel, and the albatross. They have an altogether wild and singular appearance. The true gulls of every sea are grouped in the next three cases (157-159): they come from the ice of the polar seas, and from our own shores, including the kittiwake gull, and the European black-backed gull. The last case of the gull family (160) is given to the Terns, which are caught in all parts of the world; and the Skimmers, so called from the dexterity with which they skim the surface of the water, keeping the under mandible immersed, and the upper dry, in search of prey. Next to the gulls are placed the Tropic Birds (161), the name of which indicates their native clime. These birds prey upon fish; some, as the red-tailed tropic bird, darting upon the flying-fish; and others, as the darters, boldly plunging into the tide from overhanging boughs, in search of their favourite prey; here, too, is the common Cormorant. Four more cases remain for examination, and then the visitor will have closed his inspection of the museum specimens of birds. These four cases contain, however, one or two birds, the habits of which are singular. First, there are the Pelicans with their capacious pouches. The rapidity with which these birds swallow small fish has been witnessed by most people at our Zoological Gardens. The visitor should notice next, the European Gannet, of which strange stories of strength and prowess are related. The velocity with which they dive in search of food has been variously estimated. It is said that on the coast of Scotland, fishermen have found them entangled in their nets at the extraordinary depth of a hundred and twenty feet below the surface. Pennant relates a story of a bird, which, on seeing some pilchards lying upon a floating plank, darted down with such strength, that its bill pierced the board. And now the visitor should turn to contemplate the grand and solitary Frigate Bird. This bird appears to have the power of sustaining itself in the air for an indefinite period, and to wander with the utmost confidence on its broad pinions, over hundreds of miles of ocean, now and then dipping to secure its prey. This slim, pale, and solitary wanderer must have a noble appearance, when calmly sailing upon its great expanse of wing, a thousand miles from any resting-place, its food floating in the element below, to be taken at will. Before leaving the last, or most northerly apartment of the eastern zoological gallery, the visitor would do well to notice a few of the pictures which are suspended above the wall cases. Here are portraits of Voltaire; the hardy Sir Francis Drake; Cosmo de Medici and his secretary (a copy from Titian); Martin Luther; Jean Rousseau; Captain William Dampier, by Murray; Giorgioni's Ulysses Aldrovandus; Sir Peter Paul Rubens; the inventor of moveable type, John Guttenberg (which would be more appropriately placed in the library); John Locke; a poor woman, named

Mary Davis, who in the seventeenth century, was celebrated for an excrescence which grew upon her head, and finally parted into two horns; the great Algernon Sidney; Pope; Ramsay's portrait of the celebrated Earl of Chesterfield, who, according to Dr. Johnson, "taught the morality of a profligate, and the manners of a dancing master," and a landscape by Wilson. At the northern door of this gallery are, a painting of Stonehenge, and one of the cromlech at Plas Newydd, in Anglesea.

The visitor's way now lies to the west out of the eastern zoological gallery into the most southerly of the two northern galleries. This gallery, which consists of five compartments, or rooms, is called

THE NORTHERN ZOOLOGICAL GALLERY.

The wall cases of this gallery, to which the visitor's attention should now be exclusively devoted, contain various zoological families. In the first eight wall cases of the room are distributed the varieties of Bats. These are placed here, away from the mammalia, on account of the pressure of room. They are not to be mistaken as birds in any particular. They are essentially mammalia, inasmuch as they produce their young in a breathing state and suckle them. The bats of England and other cold climates remain in a torpid condition, and only spread their wings of stretched skin when the songbirds report the advent of the warmth of spring. The visitor will notice amongst the varieties in the three first cases, the Brazilian bats, including the vampire bat (which has been known to attack a man in his sleep and suck blood from him), the remarkable leaf-nosed bats which are ranged upon the upper shelves, and the Indian and African varieties; and underneath are grouped the well-known horse-shoe bats of the eastern hemisphere. In the next case (4) are the long-eared European bats, with ears like curled leaves; and the American, African, and Australian varieties. The fifth case is filled with groups of the African and Indian taphozous; the South American tropical bats; and the West Indian chelonicteres and moormops. The last three cases, devoted to the varieties of the bat (6-8), contain those sub-families which are known as Flying Foxes, from their great size. These live on fruits, and inhabit Australia, and the southern countries of the eastern hemisphere.

The visitor's way now lies westward into the second compartment of the northern zoological gallery; for in this room, as in the rooms through which he has already passed, he should confine his attention, for the present, to the wall cases, reserving the examination of all table cases for his return visit, on his way out. And here the visitor may well pause to think upon the zoological travels he has already made, from the mammalia, which present the highest types of animal life; through the sub-families of birds, which form Cuvier's secondary class of vertebrata, or animals with a back-bone; to the threshold of the room in which the tertiary class of back-boned animals are deposited. This class includes the great families of

REPTILES,

of which there are no less than six hundred and fifty-seven varieties. Reptiles are vertebrated animals belonging to Cuvier's first great section, but distinguished from mammalia and birds, by their cold blood, their oviparous generation, and the absence of either feathers or hair from their bodies. They take precedence of fish in the animal kingdom, having lungs for aerial respiration, and "a higher circulatory organisation than the exclusive inhabitants of the water." In the museum, Cuvier's classification has been followed, with slight variations; that is to say, the reptiles have been re-divided into four classes:--the Sauria, or Lizards (in which class some modern naturalists, as Merrem and others, include serpents); the Ophidia, or Serpents; the Testudinata, or Tortoises; and the Batrachia, or Frogs. The lizards occupy the first ten wall cases in this room.

The first case contains those lizards of India and Africa which have long held the regard of eastern nations, upon the slender report that they hiss upon the approach of a crocodile, and so warn the incautious traveller to retreat in time. The truth is, these sauria prey upon the crocodile's eggs, no doubt to the particular annoyance of the crocodile, who are, therefore, it is more than probable, no friends of the monitors. The Egyptian would love the monitor for feeding upon the crocodile germ, as much as for his timely warning of the approach of the uncouth enemy. The curious heloderms, from Mexico, with their ophidian teeth, lie at the bottom of the fifth case: they are supposed, but as yet on insufficient grounds, to be poisonous. In the next case (6) are the lizards of tropical America, called safeguards. Their reputed peculiarity is that, of beating beehives till they compel the bees to retire, and then feasting upon the sweet booty: in the same case with these, is the lizard with the double-keeled tail, known as the crocodilurus. The visitor next faces a case (7) of Serpent Lizards, which do not deserve their reputation for poisonous properties, being quite harmless: here, also, are the Skinks and other varieties, including the blind worms with their hidden legs. Having dismissed the serpent lizards, the visitor will notice the Night Lizards and Guanas. The former are inhabitants of warm climates, and from the ease with which they can adapt themselves to any positions, they may be troublesome visitors; they can run with ease about the walls and ceilings of rooms, like flies; and their propensity is to roam abroad in the darkness of the night. Their broad, ugly heads, and repulsive general appearance, have won for them the character of poisonous reptiles, but the truth is they are harmless. The Crested Lizards which the visitor will notice hereabouts, are the American fruit-eating species, celebrated for violent quarrelling among themselves, and for their power of changing colour with great rapidity. They do not crawl upon the earth, but live on trees, the fruits of which sustain them. Here, too, are the Anoles, with their distended toes, that enable them to imitate the crawling feats of the night lizards. The tenth case devoted to the lizard tribe, is the most interesting of the series. It contains the family of lizards known as the Agama. This family boasts many famous scions. First, here are the Indian dragons; their resemblance to the fabled monster slain by St. George, consists of a loose skin over the ribs, which they can open or fold at pleasure. These bat-like wings will not support them in the air, but serve to steady their bodies when leaping from branch to branch of a tree. From these lilliputian representatives of the monster of fable, the visitor's attention will most probably be called by an important-looking lizard, of which Mr. Allan Cunningham brought the first specimens to this country, from Port Nelson, Australia. We allude to the lizard with a frill round its neck, which has been universally likened to that worn by Queen Elizabeth: it is called the frilled agama. It is supposed that this harmless sauroid extends this frill to frighten away its enemies; as old ladies, who can preserve their presence of mind in the neighbourhood of a bull, open their umbrella to frighten it into an opposite direction. Under these interesting sub-families are grouped the varieties of a species of agama that has won for itself an imperishable reputation--having furnished imaginative minds with matter for the most extravagant speculations--and yielded to the political writer abundant sarcastic images. No politician who has thought proper in the course of a long career, to change his old principles for new ones (as housewives exchange worn-out apparel for new gilded pottery); no philosopher who has by turns embraced conflicting principles of human action; no man of science who has published two opposite theories of the formation of our universe, can pause without emotion before this case of classed Chameleons; for the politician, the philosopher, and the man of science have inevitably figured in hostile reviews under the head of colour-changing sauroids. The popular notion respecting the colour-changing powers of these lizards is, that at will the chameleon can habit itself in any colour of the rainbow; that by turns it is a red chameleon, a blue chameleon, a green chameleon, and a yellow chameleon. The fact of the case is very far-from this notion. Chameleons are found chiefly in Africa and India, but also in some of the tropical islands. In their habits they are sluggards, lounging generally about trees, and distending their long tongues covered with a glutinous secretion, to secure passing insects, upon which they subsist. They have eyes of wonderful power, and can look backwards and forwards at the same moment; but as regards their colour, it is well to assure the visitor, that their usual tint when resting in the shade is a blue-grey, which sometimes pales to a lighter grey, turns green, assumes a brown-grey tint, or darkens to a decided brown. These are the sober observations of observant naturalists on the subject.

The class of reptiles to which the visitor should next direct his attention are those classed by Cuvier and others under the head of Ophidia, or
SERPENTS.

The particulars in which, the serpent differs from the lizard are, that the former have no feet, cast their bright coats annually (like our metropolitan postmen), and swallow their food without masticating it. They occupy seven cases. The upper part of the first case contains many of the most poisonous serpents. Among these are the well-known and formidable Rattlesnakes of America, with specimens of their rattles lying near them, which, as the visitor-will see, are a succession of osseous joints. Here too are the terrible cobra di capello, and other poisonous serpents of India; the South American fer de lance; the vipers of Europe; the North African crested viper; and the Cape of Good Hope and Western African puff adder; the Guinea nosehorn viper, and the common viper found in England--our only dangerous serpent. These serpents all inflict their poisonous wounds by means of two fangs, which they protrude from the mouth, and from the points of which they inject the poisonous matter into the wounds they inflict. On the lower shelves of this case the visitor will find some specimens of the Sea-Serpents, which frequent the East Indian seas, and the coast of New Holland. They are dangerous reptiles, having small fangs amid their teeth, with which they attack bathing animals or men. Some of them have been found sleeping on the warm bosom of a tropical ocean; and upon the warm sands of the shore they are often found, coiled up in a torpid state. They vary greatly in size: but the visitor will perceive none approaching in length to that remarkable reptile which artists, despairing in their attempts to give it the proper dimensions, lately coiled about the wide pages of pictorial papers.

The visitor will next have his attention drawn to that family of serpents of which the Boa is the great representative. These are all grouped together in cases (12-15). This family has what naturalists call "the rudiments of legs." They are a nobler family than that which the rattlesnake represents, inasmuch as they do not depend upon poison to master their enemy; but fight legitimately, with their muscular strength. The terrible pictures which adorn the pages of eastern travels for children, of poor Indians with just their heads appearing above the folds of a gigantic boa, will probably recur to the visitor, as he surveys the tortuous folds of the placid specimens of the family that lie before him. It is therefore hardly necessary to inform him that the boa family destroy their prey by coiling round it, and having secured their tail to a tree to give themselves additional strength, by crushing every bone in its body. Having thus taken the life out of the victim, the destroyer, with some trouble, if the animal be large, swallows it, and lies down for weeks to allow the process of digestion to go on. Some of these boas are from Africa, some from India, and some from America. The last two cases of serpents (16, 17) include many varieties. Here are the common water and ring snakes of England; the coach whip snakes, that live coiled about trees; the black and red ringed snakes, known as the coral snakes; and the varieties of serpents with which the famed serpent charmers of India exhibit their skill. The juggler snakes have the peculiar power of inflating the skin of the neck till it bulges over the head, and so forms a kind of hood. The Indian varieties of these hooded snakes are poisonous, and are distinguishable from the others by a yellow spot on the back of the neck.

From the serpents the visitor should turn to the families of the Testudinata, or TORTOISES.

Tortoises are broadly divided into three species, namely, land tortoises; fresh water tortoises, of which there are no less than forty-six varieties; and marine tortoises, well known to the citizens of London, in the shape of turtle-soup. The land tortoises subsist on vegetables, and are said to live occasionally more than two hundred years. The two first cases devoted to Testudinata (18, 19) contain the American, Indian, and African varieties of the land tortoise. Here is the gigantic tortoise from Galapagos, for the flesh of which many a sailor has been grateful. The visitor will remark that the shells of some of the sub-families are handsomely marked. The fresh water tortoises, having the greatest number of sub-families, occupy three cases (20-22). This species is found in the marshes or rivers of warm climates, where they prey upon small fishes and frogs. The thurgi tortoise of India, and the American snapping-tortoise, grow to a great size. In the lower part of case 22 are specimens of those tortoises which sleep with their heads bent under the margin of their shell. In the last case devoted to tortoises, are those hard tortoises known as the three-clawed terrapins of Asia, Africa, and America. These are the strictly carnivorous family that feed in the water; and may be seen preying upon the human remains that float down the Ganges. Under these terrible epicures are the marine tortoises or turtles; and among them the green turtle of the tropics. Shellfish and sea-weed are its chief food; of its flesh, all Londoners who have not tasted it, can speak pretty confidently from hearsay. It grows occasionally to a great size; those smaller ones which the citizens prize weighing generally about 600 lb. Here too are the turtle of the Mediterranean, and the hawksbill turtle of Arabia, to which ladies are indebted for the choicest of their tortoise-shell combs. Having sufficiently dwelt upon the interesting histories of the tortoises, the visitor's way lies forward in the direction of the two cases next in order of succession, which are devoted to the Loricata, or

CROCODILES.

The varieties of this family are not many; they are grouped in three cases (24-26). Here are the terrible common crocodiles which have long been the terror of the people whose native land they inhabit; the alligators, which patronise America exclusively; and the gavials of India. They are said to act as orderlies, in the rivers they frequent, devouring all the putrid matter that would else infect the atmosphere. Here too are those curious snakes which are equally thick at either end--a peculiarity which has earned for them the appellation of double-headed, and the supposed power of walking indifferently forwards or backwards. The visitor now approaches the

FROGS,
called by zoologists after the Greek name, Batrachia. The author of the Vestiges of Creation remarks, that the frog is the only animal that, like man, has a calf on the hinder part of its legs. The batrachian animals are here all grouped in one case (26). They have many peculiarities. They are in the first place almost ribless; their feet are in no way armed; many of the toads have no teeth, and those of the frog are insignificant for its size; they have no tails; neither the frogs nor the toads are venomous; the fiery expectorations of the poor toads are matters of household fable only; and their croaking choruses have startled many a poor traveller. One variety, in the case with which the visitor is now engaged, is remarkable. Here are specimens of the tree frogs that can walk with their backs downwards on the most polished surfaces, and can slightly change their colour; the paradoxical frog from Surinam, which is larger as a tadpole than in its condition of maturity; the Brazilian horned toads; the American bull frogs; and the Brazilian pipa, the female of which deposits its eggs upon the back of the male, who carries them about till they burst from their shells; the repulsive siren of Carolina, which Mr. J.E. Gray likens to an eel with fore-legs; and lastly, here is the blushing proteus, which in its native subterranean caverns is of a pale pink, but when brought to the light of day, deepens into a crimson blush; this is represented by a waxen model. It is strange that political and controversial literature, so rich in chameleons, asses in lions' skins, and other figures for human fallibility and stupidity, should not contain a few, just a few, varieties of the blushing proteus.

The visitor has now examined all the wall cases of the second room; and his way again lies to the west. The third or central room of the gallery, which he is now about to enter, is to a large class of country visitors, perhaps the most interesting apartment of the museum. Herein is deposited a complete museum of the animal life of Britain, comprehending the beasts and birds native to its soil, and the fishes that swim in its waters.

THE BRITISH ZOOLOGICAL ROOM.
In this room, as in the previous rooms, the vertebrated animals are grouped in the wall cases or on the top of the cases. It is hardly necessary to guide the visitor systematically through the intricacies of a collection, every beast, bird, fish, and shell of which is native to his own land. In the wall cases devoted to British verte-

brate animals he will notice, first the Carnivorous Beasts, which include the foxes; stoats; cats; &c.:--the Glirine Beasts, including rabbits; squirrels; hares; rats; and mice:--the Hoofed Beasts, as the fallow deer; the stag; and the roebuck:--and the Insectivorous Beasts, including moles; hedgehogs; &c.

The collection of British birds includes the Birds of Prey, as the hawks; the eagles; and the owls:--the Perching Birds, as the swallows; kingfishers; thrushes; butcher birds; rollers; and wagtails:--the Scraping Birds, as pheasants; pigeons; quails; partridges; and guinea-fowls:--the Wading Birds, including the woodcock; snipes; herons; sandpipers; storks; &c.:--and the Web-footed Birds, including swans; ducks, and sea ducks; grebes; divers; auks; petrels; gulls; gannets; cormorants; &c. The eggs of the birds are in a table case (1) and arranged like the birds.

The British reptiles are all collected in the upper part of one case, including toads; frogs; and lizards.

The British fish occupy the remainder of the wall cases. These include perch; bream; the john-dory; carp; barbel; salmon; pike; trout; sturgeon; the shark; thornback; lamprey; turbot; plaice; sole; flounder; cod; haddock; &c.

INSECTS AND SHELLS.

Three tables (2-4) are devoted to insects with jaws; the insects that are furnished with a proboscis; and a collection of British Crustacea, including lobsters; crabs; woodlice; shrimps; &c. On the table upon which the Insects with Jaws are spread, the visitor will notice many household torments, including beetles; crickets; earwigs, bees; and wasps: and in the general collection, ants; grasshoppers; cockroaches; dragon-flies; &c. The Insects with a proboscis include some beautiful butterflies with their painted wings; gnats; and, to the horror of many female visitors, bugs.

The three next tables are covered with specimens of the shells of British mollusca, or soft-bodied animals. Here are the shells of snails, cockles, mussels, oysters, &c.

The collection closes with a table case (8) which is covered with specimens of those animals called by Cuvier radiated creatures, or creatures whose nervous force is concentrated in a central point whence it radiates, as in the starfish; sea eggs, &c; corals; sea pens; corallines, &c.

Having made this rapid survey of the animal life of Great Britain from its highest to its lowest developments, the visitor should again resume his journey westward, to the fourth room of the gallery, in which the collection of

FISHES

begins. Here the Osseous or bony fishes are distributed in and on the top of the wall cases. While taking a general glance at the arrangement of the room, the visitor will at once be struck by the specimens of Sword fish--especially by the Indian flying sword fish, which are placed on the top of the wall cases on account of their length--and some of the pikes or swords of these fish, one of which, it is asserted, was driven, by the fish to which it belonged, into the hull of a stout oak ship. On the top of one of the cases the visitor should notice also the remarkable large head, from Mexico, with a long dorsal ray.

There are six orders or families of osseous or bony fish; and specimens of all these will be found in the wall cases of this room. First there is the family of

SPINY-FINNED FISHES.

This family occupies the first thirteen wall cases. Among the fishes in the first four cases, the visitor should notice the flying gurnards; the sea scorpions, and flying sea scorpions; the paradise fish; and the perches, including the fingered variety. The next cases (4-9) include, amid other varieties, the chaetodons, or bristle-toothed fish; mackarel, and horse mackarel; tunny; scombers, &c.; john-dories; and pilot fish. Then follow, next in succession, two cases (10, 11) containing the lively dolphins, which are remarkable for the rapidity with which they change colour when they are withdrawn from the water; the sturgeons, with their lancet spine; and the sea garters. The next two cases include the remaining specimens of the spiny-finned fish. Among these are the wolf fish; the curiously formed tobacco-pipe fish; the big-headed dolphins or anglers; the hand fish, with its long fins; and the rook fish.

THE SOFT-FINNED FISHES

are deposited in nine cases. In the first two cases (14, 15) of the series, are the fresh water fish of different countries, including the voracious and long-lived pike: these form an interesting group for the contemplation of anglers. The next case is devoted to hard-coated fish, as the Callichthes, which are cased with a thick scale armour; and the hard-coated Loricaria. The fish grouped in the other cases of the series, are mostly familiar to the general visitor. Here are the varieties of the salmon and the herring; cod; ling; turbot; flounders; eels of various kinds; whiting; and the lump fish. The remaining four cases of this room are devoted to a series of fishes including, in cases 23, 24, the globe fish with a parrot's beak; and the ungainly sea horses. The two last cases (25, 26) include the file fish; the coffin fishes with their hard case of octagonal plates; and the European and American sturgeons. Having examined the varieties of osseous fishes, the visitor should continue his westerly course into the fifth and last room, a compartment of the northern zoological gallery. In this room he will find the wall cases devoted to

CARTILAGINOUS FISHES.

Many of the specimens of this division are placed on the top of the wall cases, being too large to be placed inside the cases. The Cartilaginous fishes here brought together include the varieties of the ray; torpedos; and sharks. At the western extremity of this room the visitor should terminate the onward course of his first visit, and, remembering that the table cases of the northern and eastern galleries through which he has passed, remain to be examined on his way back to the grand staircase, should begin to retrace his steps, confining his attention, as he returns, to the table cases placed in the central space of the rooms through which his way lies. He should now therefore face the east, and return, in the northern zoological gallery towards its eastern extremity. The table cases deposited in the room with the cartilaginous fish are covered with

SPONGES

of different kinds. It will be interesting to the visitor to know something of the natural history of the sponge. It has been ascertained, beyond a doubt, that the sponge is an animal that sucks in its food and excretes its superfluities; that certain of its pores imbibe, while others exude; and that according to the relative positions of the two distinct sets of pores, is the shape of the sponge determined. In a natural state, as it is found in the Mediterranean, the sponge is surrounded with a thick glutinous matter, which is its vital part; like coral, it is a zoophyte: it propagates in the same manner, and its life is indestructible till it is removed from its proper element, and the glutinous matter which makes its vitality has been boiled out of its pores, leaving the soft and beautiful skeletons, of which these cases contain many specimens. Here also are some old sponges preserved in flint. Having noticed these beautiful zoophytes, the visitor should proceed in an easterly direction into the room he recently quitted, to examine the table cases it contains. The first tables to which he should direct his attention here, are those in which a series of Crustacea or hard-coated animals are deposited. They are of Cuvier's order of animal life, known as the articulata, or animals whose bodies consist of a series of moveable joints. These are mostly inhabitants of the sea, and rank in the animal kingdom as the highest class of the Articulata, except the insects, who head the order. The tables upon which the Crustacea or

SHELL FISH,

are deposited, are numbered from 13 to 24. The four first cases (13-16) are covered with Crabs of various kinds, including the long-legged spider-crabs, common crabs with oysters growing upon their backs, and fin-footed swimming crabs. The next case (17) contains in addition to the long-eyed or telescope crab, varieties of the land-crab, which is found in various parts of India; one kind, that swarms in the Deccan, commits great ravages in the rice-fields. The two next tables are covered with Chinese crabs, square-bodied crabs; those crabs with fine shells known as porcelain crabs, and the curious death's head crab, which seems to build a kind of nest of sponge or shells. But upon the next table (20) the visitor will find the most remarkable of the crabs, together with an astonishing lobster. This crab is known as the hermit crab. The visitor will perceive, that it has a long naked tail; and he should know that the one all-absorbing care of its life seems to be to find a place of safety in which this unprotected part may be screened from the dire mischances of war. Accordingly, at an early age, it sets out in search of a deserted shell into which it backs its tail; or if an unoccupied shell be not at hand, without much ceremony, the hermit contrives a summary ejectment of the lawful tenant, that it may shield its tail and be at rest. Upon the same table with this unceremonious hermit, lies the tree-lobster, which is believed to climb cocoa-trees in search of the nuts. Upon the next table (21) are the sea craw-fish and sea locusts; and upon the succeeding table (22) the visitor will remark the destructive scorpion-lobster of India, the excavations of which seriously damage the roads of that part of the world; Shrimps in all their varieties; the delicate alima, with its pale thin shell; and the long king crab. Upon the last two tables devoted to shell fish, or crustacea, are spread the goose shells or barnacles, whale lice, and I the sea acorn.

Having examined these crustacea, the visitor should turn his attention to the twelve tables (1-12) upon which a fine collection of

INSECTS

is spread. The first eight tables are covered with varieties of

THE BEETLE TRIBE.

These include some beautiful insects. The care with which the many thousand varieties have been classified by zoologists, and the minuteness with which the habits of each variety have been traced, have raised these insects to a conspicuous position in the great Animal Kingdom. Their beauty, as they lie here in vast numbers before the spectator, is dazzling. Every colour and every combination and shade of colour can be traced upon them; and in these varieties of tint there appears to be a wise provision of nature, the blue coloured beetle being the frequenter of the bark of trees, the green beetle revelling among the leaves; and the gay red and light beetles being the ***habitees*** of flower cups. Upon the first table of the series (1) are some curious varieties. Here are the remarkable burying-beetle, that deposits its eggs in the rotting flesh of small dead animals, and then, with the assistance of some kindred beetles buries the body, leaving its progeny to enjoy the carrion when they quicken; the sacred scarabaeus of the Egyptians, and the British variety of the same beetle, that bury their eggs in their dung. Upon the next table (2) are the golden tropical beetles, whose wings are used by the natives as ornaments; the celebrated glow worms, the females of which emit a phosphorescent light, in order to attract the attention of the males--thus these lights are love signals; the Brazilian diamond-beetle, a splendid insect, and the harlequin beetle. The third table (3) is covered with varieties of the kangaroo beetles, a brilliant collection of ladybirds, the varieties of earwigs, cockroaches, originally tropical insects only; the praying insects, called so from their habit of erecting their fore legs and assuming a prayerful attitude, when, in fact, they are preparing for an attack upon their prey: and the insects which the uninitiated visitor has already mistaken for pieces of stick, but which are the walking leaf-insects; some with wings like dead leaves, and others wingless. The fourth table (4) is covered with the varieties of the Cricket, including the great Chinese cricket, dragon-flies, scorpion-flies, the terrible tropical white ants, caddis flies, wasps, saw-flies, bees, hornets, and sand wasps.

BUTTERFLIES AND MOTHS.

Then follow three tables (5-7) of splendid butterflies, with their brilliant tints. The two tables (8, 9) ranged next in order to those upon which the butterflies are distributed, are covered with varieties of the moth. Here are the silkworm moth and its cocoon as kept in Siberia; the ghost moth of our hop grounds; the hawk moth, the death's head moth, and the large Brazilian owl moth.

The next table (10) is covered with a great variety of flies and bugs, including the Chinese lantern flies.

The eleventh table is given up to Spiders in all their varieties, including the tarantula, a formidable insect with a power of severe biting; and the curious spider that bores a nest in the ground, lines it sumptuously with its own silk, and then constructs a lid that closes inevitably, as the insect leaves its house. Here too are the scorpions. The last table of the series (12) is covered also with varieties of the spider, including the land and shepherd spiders; the African scarlet tick, and the centipedes. The visitor has now completed his survey of the contents of this room, and should at once pass forward in an easterly direction, traverse the British zoological room, which he has already examined throughout, and pass into the fourth room of the gallery.

The table-cases in this room present nothing that can greatly interest the unscientific visitor. They are covered with varieties of

STARFISH; SEA-EGGS, ETC.

The sea-eggs are scattered over the first nine tables (1-9) in the room. They live on small animals and sea-weed. The varieties include a flat kind, vulgarly called sea-pancakes. The remaining cases of the room are loaded with varieties of the star-fish. The mouth of the star-fish is on its lower side, through which it takes its food. It has innumerable feet, which it displays when in the water, and by means of which it can climb rocks. Some of the varieties fall to pieces on being taken from their native element, as the lizard, or brittle star-fish. The gorgon's head, which has innumerable branches from its central part, should be observed by the visitor; and the sea-wigs, which are a kind of star-fish, somewhat resembling the gorgon's head, with innumerable radii. They are placed upon table 24, near a cast of a stem and flower, that has the appearance of a fossil plant, but is in reality a cast of a crinoid star-fish that once existed in great abundance. In the most eastern room of this gallery are a few tables upon which are deposited the shells and tubes of molluscous animals, to illustrate their changes, and the way in which the animal adapts them to his position. The third and fourth tables will, perhaps, interest the general visitor. Here he will find specimens exhibiting the growth of Shells, and also how the animal repairs any damage to its shell. Here, too, are the shells upon which the modern cameo-cutters of Rome, work. As the visitor will perceive, the design is engraved in relief upon the light outer layers of the shell, leaving the darker under part exposed, as a back-ground.

The visitor's way now lies out of the northern gallery, by its eastern door, near which he should notice a remarkable sun fish, of a bulky and squat appearance. Having regained the first, or most northerly room of the great eastern zoological gallery, the visitor should turn to the south, examining the table cases of this gallery as he returns through its spacious rooms. All the table cases of this gallery, with the exception of a few small side tables, are covered with the vast varieties of the

SHELLS

of molluscous or soft animals. These shells, scattered over no less than forty-nine tables, represent the architectural capacities of the great order of soft-bodied animals, only inferior in rank, in Cuvier's "Animal Kingdom," to the Vertebrate animals.

Upon the first table, before which the visitor will find himself (49), are some interesting specimens of the well-known Cuttle fish, exhibiting its varieties, including the common cuttle fish found upon our coasts; those which have the power of secreting a dark fluid, and those from India, whose ink-bags furnish artists with that valuable brown called sepia. Here, too, are the skeletons of the slender loligos, or sea leaves, known also as sea-pens; and the crozier shell. Upon the next six tables (48-53), proceeding southward, are the varieties of the Oyster, the Mussel, and beautiful Mother-of-pearl shells. But hence the visitor will probably proceed rapidly to the south; inasmuch as the varieties of the mussel family, including the Chinese pearl mussel and Scotch pearl mussel, the borers, the club shell, and the cockle family, are not generally interesting; but he will probably linger for a few moments near the pond mussels placed upon some of the tables (38-41). The tables numbered from 24 to 30 are covered with the varieties of hard shells, which, however, present no points of interest to the general visitor, who may at once pass on to the varieties of the Nautilus and Argonaut, (tables 23, 24). And here, too, we must entreat the visitor to forget the poetic history of the inhabitants of those beautiful shells, and learn that the extended arms of the nautilus are used only to clasp its shell; that it has no sails of any kind. The varieties of the paper nautilus, or argonaut, are the most delicate and beautiful. The next table (22) displays the shell of the curious carrier, that embodies all kinds of foreign substances with its shell; the slipper shell, and the rose bud. Upon the next table (21) are the Screws; the curious ladder shells from China; and upon table 20, are the varieties of fresh water Clubs. The next two tables (18, 19) display some curious and beautiful shells, including Venus's ear, the pagoda shell, and varieties of Snails, including the apple snails. Proceeding on his southern way, the visitor should pause to notice the ear shells, placed upon tables 18, 17, including the beautiful rainbow; the button shells, the rainbow eardrop, and the pyramid upon table 16; the pomegranate from the Cape of Good Hope, New Zealand imperial, and pheasant, and the West Indian golden sun, upon table 15; the weaver's shuttle and pig cowries, including the Chinese variety, highly valued by the Chinese, as an ornament; also upon table 15, more varieties of cowries, including the money cowry of Africa, used there as money, and the orange cowry from the Friendly Islands, where it is worn as an ornament; the five varieties of the Volutes, including the red clouded volute, the Chinese imperial volute, the bishop's mitre, and the papal crown, distributed upon tables 12 and 13. The Melons, the large varieties of which are put to domestic uses by the Chinese, the olives, and butter shells, upon table 11; the magilus, whelks, and the needle shell upon table 10; the purple shell that emits the colour from which it is named, the mulberry shell, and the unicorn shell, distributed upon table 9; the tun shell, the harps, the harp helmets, and the helmets upon which cameos are carved, distributed about tables 8 and 7; the spindle shells, including the great tulip shells, and the turnip shells, occasionally used as oil-vessels in Indian temples, distributed about the tables 5, 6, and 7 are all worth examination. The splendid cone shells, which include the king of the collection, pointed out to visitors as the glory of the sea, from the Philippine Islands, and the African setting sun cone, upon tables 5 and 4; the rock shells upon table 4: the trumpet shells upon table 3, so called after the large kinds which savage tribes have been known to use as horns; and upon the last two tables, the stombs, including the beautiful varieties from the West Indies and China, close the list.

* * * * *

The visitor has now reached the Southern Extremity of the Eastern Zoological Gallery, and brought his first visit to a conclusion. He may well pause, however, before dismissing from his mind the objects which have engaged his attention.

First, then, he examined the varieties of MAMMALIA. The mammalia, of which man himself is the highest type, are the leading class of the great order of vertebrate, or back-boned animals, and fishes are the lowest, the intermediate classes being birds and reptiles. VERTEBRATA are of higher rank in the animal kingdom than the mollusca, or soft-bodied animals, those having "red blood and a double-chambered heart." The mammalia are the class which suckle their young; second to them are the BIRDS; and then the blood cools, the organisation is inferior, and the REPTILES are produced; and lastly come the FISHES, with cold blood, and wanting aerial lungs. Philosophers, who have settled the scheme of the world as one of progression, complication, or development, trace animal life from the polypus, (which belongs to the order of Radiata, or animals that have a central point in which the vital force of the animal appears to preside, diverging in radii, as in the sea-eggs, starfishes, coral, sponges); the polypus advances to the Articulata, or jointed animals, including all kinds of worms, leeches, or ringed animals, of which insects are the most highly organised developments; next to the Mollusca, or soft-bodied animals; and then from these, which include the shell-fish, the scheme gradually progresses to the fish with backbones; and here the lowest order of Vertebrata is developed: the fish merges into the reptile, the reptile into the bird; the bird, as in the ornithorhyncus, into the Mammalia.

Thus the gradations of life may be clearly apprehended by the visitor. The highest development of animal life he has seen in the MAMMALIA SALOON, all the animals of which produce their young alive and suckle them; the order of life immediately below the mammalia, he has examined in the marvellous varieties of birds arranged in the NORTHERN GALLERY; then he turned to the west, and examined the third order of animal life in the REPTILES; then the fourth order represented by FISH; and so on till he watched the simpler forms of life in the STAR-

FISH and the SPONGE.

The history of this marvellous progress of animal life, so far as scientific men have gazed into its deep mysteries, is surely worth attention. Few have the courage and the enthusiasm to follow each footstep of the tiny ant at his complex labours,--few are the Hubers that dwell among us; but to us all is given the love of that knowledge which opens our eyes to a few of the mysteries that lie thickly on our path, in the formation of the gravel upon which we tread, the clouds that grandly glide above us, and the leaves that gather upon the trees. After all the labours of our learned men, we are only now pressing, with trembling footsteps, the avenue to the endless schemes, and systems, and wonders, that lie buried in and about our world. Still let all who enter our museum, go there with the resolve to accomplish something by their visit. Even in the common concerns of life; in the petty matters that wear away the brain at last; in the market-places of the world, this insight is not without its effect. The heart is humbled as the eyes open to the grandeur of the scheme, and to the consequent littleness of individual manhood; but again, the breast swells with the purest of all pride, when the thinker says to himself: I am the King--because the hero or highest type of the Articulata, Radiata, Mammalia, or any order of vegetable or animal life. All these great and complicated developments are the beautiful works of the Great Unseen, but I am His masterpiece. One may well dream in this zoological museum, amid the staring glass-eyed skins of an inferior brotherhood--of the long, long time ago when the fossils, which are now scattered here and there, to assure us of their former vitality, moved about the world, before they were stricken with universal death, and buried by nature, deep in her teeming bosom, to flourish presently in the veins of plants--the plants to die again, and be dug, long ages after, from our deep coal-fields. These thoughts towards nature, towards the marvellous records of an antiquity, the remoteness of which we cannot realise, will rise to the minds of all visitors who can see in the vast collection of animal life through which we have guided them, revelations of the endless forms and the endless beauties that pass often unnoticed, because not understood, under every step that man takes in the many journeys that lie between his hopeful cradle and his inevitable grave.

END OF THE FIRST VISIT.

VISIT THE SECOND.

On entering the British Museum for the second time, the visitor should ascend the great staircase, pass through the south, central, and mammalia saloons; traverse the eastern zoological gallery, and continue north, direct into the first room of the most northern gallery of the northern wing;--where the studies of his second visit should begin. His first visit was occupied in the examination of the varieties of animal life distributed throughout the surface of the globe. The greater part of his time on this occasion will be devoted to the study of the wonders that lie under the surface of the earth; of the revelations of extinct animal life made by impressible rocks; and of the metallic wealth which human ingenuity has adapted to the wants and luxuries of mankind. In the fossil remains he will be able to recognise traces of an animal life, of which we have no living specimens; of trees, the like of which never rise from the bosom of the soil at the present time. The lessons that lie in these indistinct, disjointed revelations of the remote past, are pregnant with matter for earnest thought to all men. They are part of our history--links that hold us to the sources of things, and recall us again and again to the condition of our universe, as it trembled into space, and as now we inhabit it--a great and marvellous globe, every grain of which has an unfathomable story in it. Philosophers have laboured long at the story of the earth; and their revelations have tended to settle it, in a form not unlike the following:--

Originally, within the space bounded by the orbit of Uranus, a gaseous matter was diffused at a high temperature. By laws, the origin of which we have not yet traced, the condition of the diffused heat was changed, and the particles of the gaseous matter, condensed and agglomerated by attraction, into a series of planets, of which our earth is the third in point of size. That the earth has undergone vast changes, is evident to the most superficial geological student. We are only able to investigate the crust of the earth, with all our ingenious boring instruments: but even in this crust we may trace a gradual change, and recognise the silent operations of nature in ages never counted by man. According to the popular theory, the earth must have been sixty times as large as its present size, and have cooled to its present dimensions, retaining still, in its unfathomable bowels, a burning heat. The conclusions of geologists, after long and patient examination, are, that certain rocks mark the age of the world--that, in fact, the crust of the globe consists of a certain number of strata, each belonging to a certain era, as the rings of a tree tell its years of growth. The more they test this theory, the more certain are they that the history of our globe may be accurately read in the strata which compose its crust. "A granitic crust, containing vast and profound oceans, as is proved by the extent and thickness of the earliest strata, was the infant condition of the earth. Points of unconformableness in the overlying aqueous rocks, connected with protrusions of granites, and other similar presentments of the internal igneous mass, such as trap and basalt, mark the conclusions of subsequent sections in this grand tale. Dates, such as chronologists never dreamed of--compared with which, those of Egypt's dynasties are as the latter to a child's reckoning of its birthdays--have thus been presented to the now living generation, in connexion with the history of our planet."[5] These changing masses have been discovered with remains of organic life wrapped in their particles, each mass enclosing a petrified museum of the life that flourished while it was in course of formation: thus not only have we distinct proof of extinct forms of animal and vegetable life, but we are also able to assign the dates of their existence.

The MOST EASTERLY ROOM of the NORTHERN MINERAL and FOSSIL GALLERY, is that to which the visitor's attention will be first directed. In this room, as in the next three, the table cases are devoted to the minerals; and the wall cases, along the southern side of the gallery, are filled with

FOSSIL VEGETABLES.

The wall cases of this room contain the various strata which have traces of vegetable life. The earliest vegetable life of which the geologist has found fossil remains is in the form of sea-weeds, specimens of which the visitor will notice in case 1. The grand harmony of the world's development is shown in this adaptation of the earliest vegetable life to that of the earliest animal life--the polypus drawing its sustenance from the sea-weed. In the next three cases the visitor will notice various remains of fossil ferns (in clay slate) and horse-tails, all indicating the former high temperature and moisture of the localities in which they are found, since they are of large proportions, and it is observable that these plants grow in bulk according as they near the tropics. That the ferns and club mosses have diminished with the decrease of temperature of the earth, is proved by comparing the fossil club mosses, which have been found as large as beech trees, whereas at the present time the most gigantic club moss rarely exceeds three feet in height. In the lower sections of the third, fourth, and fifth cases, the visitor may notice some fine specimens of polished fossil woods; but the varieties of vegetable fossils can hardly engage his serious attention for any length of time, unless he have some real knowledge of botany and geology; yet he may gather the solemn teaching that lies in those dark masses of early coal formation and clay slate, even though he be unable to explain the first principles of botanical science. He may notice, however, in the fifth and sixth wall cases, fossil specimens of extinct plants, including the sigillaria, which, when living, is supposed to have attained often to the height of seventy feet. Having noticed these vegetable remains, the visitor should cross to the northern wall of the room, and examine the sandstones upon which the tracks of an extinct animal called the chirotherium--and footprints, supposed to be of birds, are distinguishable.

The central object in the room is a tortoise found in Hindostan, near Allahabad. It is carved out of nephrite or jade, and is deposited upon a curious table of inlaid ancient marbles. Against the eastern wall are deposited some beautiful varieties of branched native silver from Norway; Lady Chantrey's specimen of part of a coniferous tree, semi-opalised; and a mass of websterite from Newhaven, Sussex. The table cases now remain for examination. These are devoted to varieties of

MINERALS.

and their combinations. The visitor should examine the cases in the order in which they are arranged, beginning with the cases marked 1 and 1A. These two cases contain specimens of native Iron. Native iron has nearly always proved to be of meteoric origin; and the specimens are here arranged in the order in which they have been found. They have fallen from the heavens at different places, and at different periods. The largest known aerolite is that which fell in Brazil, and was no less than eight feet in length. These huge solid masses of iron, discharged from the clouds in a burning state, may well set the brains of philosophic men to work, to unravel the splendid mystery that contrives laboratories high up in the air, from which dense tons of pure iron are discharged upon our earth. Humboldt, discarding the Laplaceian theory that aerolites were detached masses of the moon, which ignited on reaching the oxygen that surrounds our globe, asserts that they are Lilliputian planets, having their system as we have ours; that they are identical with shooting stars, and that they occasionally fall to the earth by coming within the attraction of a body of overpowering magnitude. In the case with these meteoric specimens of native iron are specimens of native Copper--not often found in a pure state; native Lead, of meteoric origin; one specimen, exhibited in the form of a medal, having been cast out of the crater of Vesuvius about two hundred years ago; and native Bismuth, which expands as it cools.

In the second case the visitor will particularly notice the beautiful threads of native Silver from the Hartz Mountains; and the various forms in which pure silver is found; native Mercury, and combinations of mercury and silver called native amalgam, some moulded into figures by Mexican miners; native Platinum from Siberia; and Palladium.

The third case of the series is resplendent with samples of native Gold--a metal that plays so powerful a part in the affairs of men--that has roused the fiercest passions of mankind, and been coveted by human beings from the remote times when the Phoenicians dreamt of golden lands in the east. Half of this table case is covered with native gold and alloys. Pure gold is generally found in separate crystals or grains, but the metal is mostly found combined with other substances. It is alloyed, for manufacturing purposes, with copper and silver.

Half of the third case, and cases 4, 5, and 6 in this room, are covered with various electro-negative metals and metalloids, classed according to the system laid down by Berzelius. In the third case are Tellurium and Tellurets. In the fourth are samples of native Arsenic, and its combinations with nickel and cobalt; Carbon in its various forms, pure as in the diamonds, which the visitor will notice attentively, some imbedded in the earth in which they were discovered, and models of celebrated diamonds; Black Lead in porcelain earth, for which Cumberland is celebrated; Selenium in its combinations with lead, mercury, sulphur, and other metals; and a medallion, in selenium, of Berzelius, who discovered this metal in 1818. The sixth case is covered with Sulphurets, chiefly of iron, these being commonly known as iron pyrites. These specimens of the commonest of metallic ores are from various parts of the world. Upon this table also are deposited Lord Greenock's sulphuret of cadmium, commonly called greenockite; and sulphurets of nickel. Having examined the first six cases of the series ranged along the southern side of the room, the visitor should turn to the six last cases of the series (55-60). The first northern case (55) is covered with various Sulphates, or metals in combination with sulphuric acid, exhibiting beautiful crystals and colours, including sulphate of magnesia from Oregon; sulphate of zinc, or white vitriol; sulphate of iron, or green vitriol; and the splendid blue sulphates of copper from Hungary; beautiful sulphates of lead from Anglesea; sulphates of alumina; common alum; and the splendid specimens of lazurite, or lapis-lazuli,--

"Blue as the veins o'er the Madonna's breast,"

from which the beautiful pigment called ultramarine is extracted. In 1828 M. Guimet succeeded in making an artificial ultramarine, known now extensively as French ultramarine, which is little, if at all, inferior in beauty to lazurite. The next case (56) contains the Arseniates, including arseniate of lime, crystallised; arseniates of copper; arseniate of nickel; and red cobalt, or arseniate of cobalt. The next case is devoted to the Phosphates, or metals mixed with phosphoric acid, including crystals of the phosphate of iron from Fernando Po, Bavaria, and Cornwall; phosphates of manganese; phosphate of copper; yellow and green uranite; phosphates of alumina, including the blue spar, which has been mistaken for lapis-lazuli, and the phosphate of alumina known as turquois, found only in Persia, and esteemed as an ornament. In the two supplemental table cases, 57 A and B, the visitor may notice specimens of Pyromorphite, a combination of phosphate and chloride of lead, and a combination of chloride of calcium with phosphate of lime. These combinations, however, cannot interest the general visitor.

The case marked 58 contains the varieties of Fluorides, or combinations of fluorine and the metals. These include the fluoride of calcium, of which the most familiar variety to Englishmen is that known as Derbyshire spar, of which many useful articles are manufactured in this country. Ladies particularly will halt with interest before the case marked 58 A, where the fluorides, better known as the topaz, are deposited. These include a fine series of crystals from the Brazils, Siberia, and Saxony.

The 59th case is covered with Chlorides, or combinations of chlorine with other substances, including rock salt, or chloride of sodium; sal-ammoniac from Vesuvius; fine chloride of copper, exhibiting beautiful crystals; and chlorides of silver and mercury. The two last cases in the room (60 and 60 A) contain samples of coal, bitumen, resins, and salts. Here will be found the honey-stone of Thuringia; crystals of phosphate of magnesia and ammonia called struvite; beautiful specimens of amber, some pieces of which inclose insects; and copal, also containing insects; fossil copal; mineral pitch, from naphtha to asphalt; the elastic bitumen of Derbyshire, exhibiting its different degrees of softness; Humboldt's dapeche, an inflammable fossil of South America; and brown and black coal. Having noticed all these varieties, the visitor should advance at once westward into the second room of the mineralogical gallery.

Here, against the southern wall, are groups of

FOSSIL ANIMALS

ranged inside and upon the top of the wall cases. The most remarkable of the remains inclosed in the wall cases of this room are the remains of the carapace and other portions of the gigantic Fossil Tortoise from the Sewalik Hills, Bengal, discovered by the enterprising Major Cautley; and the gigantic fossil bones of an extinct genus of birds that inhabited New Zealand in the remote past. But these wall cases are mainly devoted to the exhibition of chelonian, or tortoise fossils, which are the highest class of fossil reptiles, except the serpents, and found only in the later or oolite formations of the earth. The regularity with which the various families of reptiles are discovered in the earth's strata, according to their order, is remarkable. First the Lizards are found in the magnesian limestone, immediately above the coal deposit, indicating their early appearance on the earth; the next deposit, or new red sandstone, introduces us to the Frogs; the oolite to the Tortoises; and the recent tertiary strata to the Serpents. The bones of the tremendous wingless birds, which are deposited in the third case of this room, have been recognised by Professor Owen as the remains of an animal that must, when living, have stood eleven feet high. By the windows in the northern wall of the room are deposited the beautiful crystallised mass of Selenite, or sulphate of lime, found in the duchy of Saxe Coburg, and presented to the museum by Prince Albert; and a mass of carbonate of lime, presented by Sir Thomas Baring. Having noticed these prominent attractions of the room, the visitor should direct his attention to the table cases, and first to those ranged along the southern half of the room (7-13). Five of the tables are loaded with further specimens of the Sulphurets, or metals in combination with sulphuric acid. In the first case (7) are sulphurets of copper, and copper iron; in the second case (8) are the series of sulphurets of lead, or galena, from various parts of the world; in the third case (9) are specimens of sulphuret of bismuth, needle ore, or sulphuret of bismuth, copper, and lead, and sulphurets of mercury, or cinnabar, chiefly from Spain, the light variety of which is the bright vermilion used by artists; in the fourth case (10) are the sulphurets of silver, the beautiful crystallised sulphurets of antimony, chiefly from Transylvania, and the delicate plumose antimony, or feather ore; in the fifth case (11) are the sulphur salts, including the ruby, silver, &c.; and in the sixth case (12) are the sulphurets of Arsenic, red orpiment, of which the best comes from Persia, cobalt glance, &c., bringing the series of sulphurets to a conclusion.

In the next case (13) the series of Oxides begins. Herein are the oxides and hydrous oxides of manganese.[6] Having examined the sulphurets and oxides, the visitor should cross to the northern suite of tables marked from 48 to 54. Here are arranged a series of the Carbonates, or combinations of carbonic acid with earths, metallic oxides or alkalis.

In the first case (48) are some specimens of brown spar from Hungary, fibrous and crystallised carbonates of iron, and manganese spar; in the second case (49) are the varieties of zinc spar, or carbonates of zinc, lead spar, or carbonates of lead, and carbonates of bismuth and cerium; in the third and fourth cases (50, 51) are the carbonates of copper, the 51st case containing those splendid green carbonates of copper from the mines in the Uralian Mountains, known commonly as Malachite, and when in a polished state vulgarly mistaken for a green and beautifully veined marble. Most visitors on examining these lumps of malachite will think of the beautiful colossal furniture manufactured of it by the Russians, and exhibited by them in their department of the Great Exhibition. The next three cases (52-54) are filled with series of sulphates, and some nitrates, including native nitre, or saltpetre. The Sulphates in the cases include glauber salt, or sulphate of soda; heavy spar or sulphates of baryta, among which are some splendid crystallisations from Piedmont, Hungary, Spain, and other countries; sulphate of strontia, known also as celestine, among which are some delicate blue crystals from Sicily; sulphates of lime, as gypsum, including some fine specimens of alabaster, and the fibrous sulphate known vulgarly as tripe-stone. The visitor has now examined the contents of the second room; the fossil tortoises and great wingless birds; the mineral combinations--nearly all of which are useful to man; and the way westward may be resumed to the third department of the northern mineralogical gallery. In the wall cases of this room are deposited some of the most interesting

FOSSIL ANIMALS.

Of these the celebrated fossil Salamander (which a German enthusiast mistook for a fossil human skeleton), deposited in the first case, will probably be most attractive to the general visitor. The first three wall cases are devoted to the batrachian or Frog fossils; some of the chelonian or Tortoise fossils; and the fossil crocodiles. Fossil lizards are the most numerous of all fossil remains. Of these, including the fossil crocodiles, the visitor will notice specimens in the wall cases of this room, indicating the enormous size to which these extinct reptiles must have grown. One, the Iguanodon (case 3) was an animal that measured seventy feet in length. It existed in this country; various bones of it are in this case. The remains of the fossil Alligator, known as the mosasaurus, are also here, together with the wealden lizard of Kent, which was about twenty-five feet in length, and part of Cuvier's wonderful fossil Flying Lizard, or sterodactylus, which is described as a reptile having mammalian characteristics, a bat's wings, enormous eyes, and a bird's neck. In the westerly cases of the room the visitor should notice the fossil sea lizards divided into two families--the Plesiosaurus, and the Ichthyosaurus. The plesiosaurus was an extraordinary reptile, of gigantic size, the length of whose neck exceeded that of its body and tail. It had ribs like a chameleon, and the body of a whale: it chiefly inhabited the water; but as the visitor will find the chief types of these extraordinary extinct reptiles in the next room, he may at once, with the comfortable assurance that the Weald of Kent yields nothing in the present day like the wealden lizard, turn to the table cases of the room, in which he will find further varieties of

MINERALS.

The southern range of tables is numbered from 14 to 23; and the northern range from 38 to 47. The first three tables of the southern range (14-16) are covered with the varieties of Oxides of Iron, including magnetic iron ore; natural magnets;

the salam-stell of the East Indies; iron glance from Elba, Vesuvius, and Stromboli, some of which are very beautiful; brown iron stones, including the variety used as hair powder by natives of South Africa; and the pea ores that fell in a shower, on the 10th of August, 1841, in Hungary. In the next case (17) are the Oxides of Copper; bismuth; red oxide of zinc; cobalt ochres; oxide of uranium; and pitch ore. In the nineteenth case are the Oxides of Lead; and in the twentieth are the first of the oxides of electro-negative substances. This case contains the valuable alumina known as noble corundite, and to jewellers in its formations of ruby, sapphire, and the oriental emerald, topaz, and amethyst. Herein also is the kind of corundum known as emery, and esteemed for its polishing properties. In this case also are the Aluminates of Magnesia, including the sapphirine; the chrysoberyls from Brazil, and those inclosed in quartz and felspar with garnets. The next four cases (20-23) are loaded with the varieties of the Acid of Silicium or silica, which constitutes the greater part of hard stones and minerals with which the earth is encrusted. It is nearly pure in the rock crystal, of which there are many specimens in the first case (20), including those crystals called Bristol and Gibraltar diamonds, cairngorms, the smoky topaz; rock crystals inclosing foreign substances, and in a wrought state: of these Dr. Dee's snow-stone is one. The next two cases (21, 22) are devoted to the varieties of common quartz, including the flexible sandstones of Brazil (of which there are some larger specimens upon a separate table) and to those of the east; milk quartz; the Salzburg blue quartz, &c.; some varieties of the cat's eye; hornstones, including wood changed into hornstone: and herein begin the flints, including some specimens changing into calcedony, smalt blue calcedony from Transylvania; the Icelandic stalactical calcedony; and the fine Cornish calcedony. Upon the last southern table (23) are ranged further varieties of calcedony. These include the blood stone; the curious Mocha stones; and agates, including the agate nodule from central Asia. Having sufficiently examined these beautiful varieties of calcedony, the visitor should pass at once to the northern range of tables.

Upon the first of these tables (38) are some new scientific varieties of mineral substances, in which the unscientific visitor will not take any interest; herein also are Oxides of Antimony, including white antimony from Bohemia; red antimony, or kermes, not to be mistaken for the ancient dye used by the old Greek and Roman dyers, which was obtained from the female *coccus illicis*; and tungstates of lime, lead, and of iron and manganese.

In the second case (39) are the Molybdates and molybdic acid; the Chromates, including red lead ore from the Siberian gold mines of Beresof; chromate of lead and copper, and crome iron from Var, in France;--the Borates, including borates of magnesia, and borate of soda, or borax. In the third case (40) are some remarkable varieties of silicates, which contain borates from Norway and other countries; and in the fourth case (41) are the first in order, of the carbonates, including carbonates of soda, the beautiful crystals of carbonate of baryta, carbonate of strontia and aragonites, from Aragon, Hungary, Bohemia, and Vesuvius; and in the next case (42) are deposited further varieties of aragonite, and some remarkable varieties of calcite, or carbonate of lime. The next three cases (43-45) are chiefly devoted to the various crystallisations of calcite, including that generally known as the Fontainbleau crystallised sandstone, and the stalactic and fibrous varieties from Africa, Sweden, and Cumberland; while the two cases marked 45 A and B are covered with polished samples, known to people generally as marbles, including the beautiful fire marble. The forty-sixth case is also covered with calcites, including the reastone, the limestone incrusted upon a human skull, found in the Tiber at Rome. In the 47th case are varieties of carbonate of magnesia, and magnesian limestone, including a remarkable one from Massachusetts. Some marble tables are also in this room, placed here to exhibit the beauties of various calcites. The table of Serpentine is here: also the table inlaid with porphyries; one with a series of bivalve shells (25); and in the centre of the room is the stalagmitic table, from the Blythe lead mine, Derbyshire, with black marble legs from Bakewell, given to the trustees of the Museum by the Duke of Rutland. Before leaving this room the visitor should not fail to notice the Maidstone Iguanodon deposited in a bed of sandstone, and placed beneath the central north window of the room. The bones are disjointed, but the general form of the reptile may be more perfectly seen here than in any other fossil remains of the iguanodon. Having noticed this fossil, and remarked the classed groups of gigantic dark fossil bones, which cover the southern wall, the fossil turtles from Sussex and other parts, and the great fossil thigh bones of reptiles that have passed long since from the face of the earth, the visitor should once more advance into the fourth room of the gallery.

In this room the wall cases are devoted to

FOSSIL ANIMALS.

Of these the most interesting specimens are the remains of the Marine Lizards known as ichthyosauri from the English lias formation. To the right on entering, against the eastern wall of the room, the visitor should first notice the fossil remains of various carnivorous animals, including the skulls and other osseous wrecks of hyenas, bears, &c., and also, carefully screened in an additional glass case, hereabouts, the lower jaw of a marsupial animal on a slab of oolitic limestone--an early deposit, in which the highest class fossils generally found are the tortoises.

In this room, however, the visitor will notice the progress of early creation-- first, the zoophytes; then the fish lizards; then the fossil ruminants; then the fossil carnivora. Examples of these fossil remains are all included in the room which the visitor has now reached. First, he should examine the fossil remains of the ichthyosauri, or fish lizards, ranged in the first three wall cases, particularly that eighteen feet in length, deposited in the third case, one on the upper shelf of the fourth case, and another on the upper shelf of the fifth case. The case marked F contains fossils of a higher order than the reptiles, as the bones and antlers of deer, found in later strata of the earth's crust; and on the top of the case are the horn and skull of a species of Texan bos. Having noticed these curious remains, principally of extinct species of animal life, the visitor should at once turn to the table cases which contain the last of the illustrations of the mineral kingdom.

MINERALS.

The southern tables include the numbers 24 to 30. The first table contains a very attractive collection of minerals, including the varieties of jasper; all kinds of opals--the sun opal, the semi-opal, wood opal, and wood partially opalised. The second table (25) is covered with varieties of Silicates of Lime, magnesia, and alumina; also soapstone, keffekil, or the meerschaum, highly esteemed by smokers, serpentine, chrysolite, &c. The third case (26) is devoted to Silicates of Zinc, magnesia, serium, copper, iron, bismuth, and other minerals; the fourth and fifth cases (27, 28) to zoolitic substances; the sixth case (29) to various minerals including samples of jade or nephrite, of which the tortoise, in the first room of this gallery, is manufactured; and the seventh case (30) to felspathic substances, including amazon stone from the Urals, and Labrador felspar. The northern cases are numbered from 31 to 37. In the first case (31) are varieties of felspar; in the second case (32) are micaceous and other mineral substances; in the third case (33) are basaltic hornblende, tremolite, &c.; in the fourth case (34) are varieties of asbestus, which defies the action of fire; jeffersonite; jenite from the Elba, &c.; in the fifth case (35) are various pyroxenic minerals; in the sixth case (36) are various kinds of garnets, including the lime and chrome varieties; and in the 37th case are the silicates, including beryls, and the emerald.

Having brought his examination of the mineral kingdom to a conclusion, the visitor should notice the fossil zoophytes and shells from various deposits, arranged upon the other tables of the room. He will now leave the mineral kingdom, and advancing once more westward, will reach the fifth room of the gallery, which is entirely given up to various fossil remains.

FOSSIL FISHES

The first object that will arrest the visitor's attention on entering this fine apartment is the gigantic skeleton of the extinct elk of Ireland, which towers above every other object, from its pedestal, placed in the centre of the room. It is seven feet in height, and eight feet in length.

The southern wall cases and the southern table cases of this room are covered with the fossil remains of various fishes. These are important to the student as exhibiting high forms of animal life that existed at the time of the formation of the most ancient strata in which organic remains have been discovered. The visitor will notice the perfect forms imprinted upon the various strata here exhibited.

In case 7 he will be struck with the fossil remains of some of the sauroids or lizard-like fishes, only two species of which survive to the present day, but which, in remote ages, abounded in the seas, and were particularly voracious. On the middle shelf of the wall case marked B the visitor should notice the fossil remains of the enormous and powerful carnivorous fish called the rhizodus; also the macropoma, like a carp in shape, in wall cases 13, 14; the fossil bremus in case 19; the extinct species of fossil carps, in cases 24, 25; the fossil pikes in cases 24-27; and the fossil herrings in the middle of cases 25-27. Having noticed these fossils the visitor should examine the wall case in the north-eastern corner of the room in which are deposited many bones of mammalia from the Sewalik Hills, including the teeth and jaws of an extinct species of camel; and the skull of the remarkable livatherium; and on the top of the case are various bones of the same extinct monster. The tops of the southern cases display various fossil remains, including the head-bones of the asterolepis; the skull and antlers of the Irish elk; and various skulls of different kinds of oxen. The western wall case is filled with a curious collection of various fossil parts of an extinct species of rhinoceros found in this country, also skulls of the rhinoceros dug up in Siberia. There is something impressive in the effect--the atmosphere of this and the sixth rooms. As crowds of holiday people, inhabitants of an island in which no dangerous living animals now abide, wander amid the fossil remnants of ages when the most terrible monsters must have lived in British waters and crawled upon British ground, curious contrasts rise in the brains of contemplative men. The mind wanders back to the age of reptiles--to times when no human footprint had sunk into the earth--and the great agents of nature were silently depositing in the congregating and shifting earths dead images of the prevailing life. Ages roll on as the reptiles give place to higher animal organisation developed in carnivora, the quickening blood warms, and then as the sovereign of all the grades of life, erect and gifted with reason, comes man. Something of this vast and half-told progress is shown in the range of fossil cases with which the visitor is engaged. He has passed the era of reptiles and fishes, and on entering the sixth and last room of the gallery, he will notice the higher series of fossils. The distribution of the

FOSSIL MAMMALIA

in this room is very striking; the central space being fully occupied by the cast of the wonderful megatherium of the Pampas, and the skeleton of the North American mastodon. The megatherium is described zoologically as having combined the characteristics of the armadillo, sloth, and ant-eater. In height it averaged eight feet; its feet were a yard in length; and its claws were of terrible strength; it was encased in an impenetrable scaly armour; and it lived upon roots. The mastodon was of the elephant kind. But the gigantic tapir described by Baron Cuvier, or the dinotherium, supposed by the Baron to have reached the extraordinary height of eighteen feet, of which only partial remains have been found, and are here deposited, is the largest fossil mammalia yet discovered. It is said to have had the habits of the walrus. The southern wall cases of the room contain a fine collection of the fossil remains of elephants and mastodons, chiefly from the Sewalik Hills of northern India. The third case (c) is filled with Brazilian fossils of varieties of the megatherium, monkeys, &c. On the right of the entrance from the fifth room are some fossil mammalia from Montmartre arranged by Cuvier. Having wandered about amid these suggestive wrecks of the remote past, the visitor should approach the central upright case placed against the western wall of this noble room. Here is a fossil of part of a human skeleton, the possession of which our geologists owe to the fortune of war--it having been found on board a French ship captured by an English cruiser. As the visitor will perceive, the skull is wanting, but this important part is said to lie in an American museum. However, the spine, the thigh bones, and the ribs are distinctly visible. This precious relic was extracted, with other human fossils, from the cliffs of Guadaloupe, about forty years ago. It is the skeleton of a savage slaughtered about one hundred and fifty years ago, and buried in the spot where it was found. As yet, the period when man first appeared upon the face of the earth is not told in geology. No fossil human remains have been found even in the ancient tertiary strata. The story of human life is revealed in other records, if not in the sepulchral strata of the earth's crust. In this very Museum, which the visitor now treads--in these cases of fossil bones which in themselves are common material enough, the lordly intellect that has traced their deep significance, proves that, of all animal types, man is the highest and the strongest--removed from the most powerful mammoth and megatherium--the bones of which he has re-fixed, that they may, as stones, tell the story of their wonderful characters when alive. A curious resurrection this, by Cuvier and others, of long ages ago, to be pondered well. Not a holiday matter, to be stared at--an hour's wonder--and then forgotten, as of no value in the markets of the living world; but a great and a serious science, with more romances in it than shelves of novels. To know something of the early state of the world which we enjoy--to have some evidences given to us that before human animals began to play their part here, wonderful monsters, part mammalia, part birds, part reptiles, gambolled upon the scene; that wingless birds stalked upon marshy grounds; that strange and ghastly lizards crawled upon our fruitful Kent; and gigantic fish floated in our tranquil waters, but no beautiful humming birds, majestic lions, and graceful horses--only crawling and swimming life, everywhere preying, and the early sea-weed rising in the sea because the polypus wanted its food: to think of these things is to have some knowledge. In these dim regions of the past, what glimpses are there of the great eternal laws, the natural progresses, the continual upward tendency of all things! And then, taking this revealed book of the past in his hand, how a man may sit and ponder on all that is to be--dream of times when some future geological hammer will be rapping at the clay about the stone relics of his bones, and a man will gaze upon his hardened anatomy with a mild and holy joy--when all that breathes and moves to-day will be entombed in ancient strata of the earth, and busy life will be carried on a hundred feet above the ruins of the present. These thoughts dwell happily with good men.

Hence, proceeding on his way, the visitor returns east from the sixth room into the fifth, and turns thence south, into the passage which leads into the western gallery of the Museum, and immediately into

THE EGYPTIAN ROOM.

This room is always an attractive part of the Museum to the majority of visitors. Here are arranged illustrative specimens of the arts and customs of people who lived two thousand years before our era; and the preserved bodies of men and women who trod the streets of Thebes and Memphis, partakers of an advanced civilisation, when the inhabitants of Europe were roaming about uncultivated wastes, in a state of barbarism. Here are graceful household vessels, compared with the art of which the willow pattern of the nineteenth century is a barbarism, and fabrics of which modern Manchester would not be ashamed. Into this room a vast collection of Egyptian curiosities is crowded; and, with patience, the visitor may glean from an examination of its contents a vivid general idea of the arts and social comforts of the ancient people who built the Pyramids, and were in the height of their prosperity centuries before the Christian era. The cases are so divided and sub-divided that it is only by paying particular attention to the numbers marked upon them that the visitor can hope to follow our directions with ease. He will see, however, on first entering the room, that the mummies are placed in cases occupying the central space of the room; and that huge and gaudily painted coffins, having a somewhat ghastly effect, are placed perpendicularly here and there on the top of the wall cases. But the attention of the visitor on entering this room is usually rivetted at once upon the human remains of people that flourished more than two thousand years before our era. The first thought that rises in the mind of the spectator on beholding these wrecks of the human form, is,--why all this trouble, these bandages, these scents, and these ornaments? It is as well, therefore, to explain that the ancient Egyptians believed that there would be a resurrection of the body hereafter. They believed that these poor mummies would issue from these waxen bandages, and once more walk and talk as of old; hence their gigantic excavations at Thebes for secure tombs; hence the great Pyramids built to preserve the sacred forms of their Pharaohs. Some of the ancient Egyptians retained the embalmed bodies of their relations in their houses, enclosed in coffins, upon which the face of the deceased was faithfully pourtrayed. Some specimens of these representations are in the room, and some in the Egyptian saloon below. The mummies of the poorer classes were not so well preserved as those of the rich; therefore, remains of the plebs have crumbled to dust, while those of the sacerdotal class, having been deprived of the intestines, and the brain having been drawn through the nose, having been filled with myrrh, cassia, &c., soaked in natron,[7] and then securely bandaged, have remained in a comparatively sound state to the present time, and may be found in every museum of any note.

HUMAN MUMMIES.

The first five cases to which the visitor would do well to direct his attention are those marked from 46 to 50. In the first division is deposited the mummy of a female, with a gilt mask over the head and an oskh or collar about the neck; and mummies of children, and fragments of coffins, with paintings of Egyptian deities upon them. In the second division of the cases, lies some of the kingly dust of the builder of the third pyramid, King Mencheres; also, part of his coffin; the sides of a coffin decorated with drawings of deities; clumps of mummied hair; and mummies of children. In the third division are tesserae from Egyptian mummies of the Grecian period, with various figures, including one of Anubis, the embalmer of the dead; a mummy of Amounirion covered with a curious network of bugles in blue porcelain; the upper part of a coffin with dedications to the Egyptian god Osiris; a small coffin containing the mummy of a child; the mummy of a female, Auch-sen-nefer, upon which is a scarabaeus, the sacred beetle of the Egyptians. In the fourth division the principal object is the coffin of the last-named mummy, with representations of various deities, including Nutpe, or the Abyss of Heaven, a female figure with a vase on her head; and linen wrappers from mummies of the Greek period. Having examined these human relics of remote antiquity, the visitor should pass at once to cases 63, 64, leaving the intermediate cases for future examination, where he will find scraps and fragments of the coffins, wrappers, and ornaments of various mummies. In the first division are fragments of the mask of mummy coffins; fragments from the lower end of coffins with the Egyptian bull Apis carrying a mummy upon it; and hands (one holding a roll) from mummy coffins; sepulchral sandals, one with a foreign figure bandaged, in token of the enemies of the deceased being at his feet. In the second division are a variety of sepulchral tablets to Osiris, Isis, Anubis, and other Egyptian deities. The next twelve cases are filled with human mummies and their coffins. In the first case is a mummy (1) of Pefaakhons, an auditor of the royal palace during the twenty-sixth dynasty. This mummy is about two thousand two hundred years old. Upon it the visitor may notice the representation of Egyptian deities Osiris, the Hawk of Ra, Isis, the embalmer Anubis, and the bull Apis. Mummy number two, in this case, is that of a priest of Amoun, Penamoun, swathed in its bandages, and here also is the outer linen case of the mummy of Harononkh. The next case (66) is devoted to the mummy and coffin of Tatshbapem: the figures here represented are the deceased praying to Osiris, the usual figure of the embalmer of the dead, Anubis, and a scarabaeus, or sacred beetle, made of beads. The next case contains the coffin and mummy of a priestess of Amoun, named Kotbti. The hair is attached to the mask of the face, as the visitor will observe, by two ivory studs: there are wooden models of the hands and arms decorated with bracelets and rings; each hand upon the coffin holds a nosegay, and here again the black Anubis with, his golden face appears in company with Thoth (a figure of a man with the head of an ibis), the Mercury of the Egyptians, god of the moon and inventor of speech, Isis, the Egyptian Ceres, and Nutpe, the Abyss of Heaven. The next case (68) is the highly decorated coffin of the incense-bearer of the abode of Noumra. Here the judgment scene of the Amenti is pourtrayed; Osiris, in the shape of a sphinx; and other sacred figures. The following case (69) contains a mummy (1) of a Theban priest of Amoun, swathed in its outer linen coverings, which are decorated with various Egyptian divinities, and with Asiatic captives at the feet: the second object in this case is the coffin of an incense-bearer of the temple of Khons, with the usual representations of the sepulchral deities. Advancing in the regular order in which the cases are numbered, the visitor will next notice in case 70 the inner coffin of a supposed Egyptian king, with the bandages with inscriptions at the side. Three mummies are placed in the next case (71) the first of which is crumbling rapidly, the feet being already gone: and the bandages of the second present pictures of Anubis embalming the deceased, and Isis mourning over the ceremony. The next four cases (72-75) are also filled with mummies and their appendages, of which the mummy and coffin of a sacred functionary with a gilded face, and a picture of the deceased adoring King Amenophis the First, in the 73rd case, and the mummy and coffin of a musician of the Roman era of Egypt in case 74 are the most remarkable. The last case of mummies (76) contains three mummies. The first is that of a priestess of Amoun, whose form is discernible through the bandages, the feet of which are visible, and the third is that of a woman named Cleopatra, of the family of Soter, Archon of Thebes, with a comb in the hair, and upon the bandages the usual sepulchral deities, including the black Anubis, and in the next case is her coffin.

The visitor having completed his survey of the human mummies should return to the series of cases marked from 52 to 58, in which he will find a curious assortment of

ANIMAL MUMMIES.

Animal life was venerated by the Egyptians. Certain animals were sacred in certain parts of the country; but the ibis and the hawk were generally worshipped. The sacred birds were attended to by the priests. Seven cases in this room are entirely filled with the mummies of these sacred birds. Here are mummies of dog-headed baboons, worshipped at Hermopolis, and sacred to Thoth; a head of the cynocephalus from Thebes; mummies of jackals, sacred to the sepulchral Anubis; the head of a dog in bandages, and one with the bandages unrolled. Mummies of oats, the female being sacred to the goddess Pasht, or Diana, and the male to the sun; a wooden figure of a cat containing the mummy of one; and bronze cats from the cat mummy pits of Abouseir. In the fifty-fourth and fifty-fifth cases are mummies of parts of bulls; gazelles; unrolled heads of rams; and the mummy of a lamb. In the two following cases (56, 57) are a variety of mummies of the ibis, perhaps, the most sacred bird of the Egyptians, and the emblem of Thoth: these include Sir J. G. Wilkinson's present of the black ibis and two eggs; and conical pots containing mummies of the ibis. The last case (58) contains some strange mummies, including those of crocodiles, emblematic of the Egyptian Sevek, the subduer; mummies of snakes sacred to Isis, in the shape of circular cakes; and in case 60, the visitor may notice more specimens of mummy snakes and fish. The next two cases are filled with the specimens of some dried birds of ancient Egypt, some stamped with the names of Sesostris, Amenophis, and Thothmes; and some from the Pyramids of Illahoun, Howara, and Dashour. The visitor should now direct his attention to the large collection of

EGYPTIAN SEPULCHRAL AND OTHER ORNAMENTS.

These are interesting as illustrative of the Egyptian art of remote period. These fragments occupy no less than twenty-four cases (77-102). In the first case (77) the visitor should notice the coffin of the mummy Cleopatra, ornamented on the outside with ordinary emblematical drawings and on the inside with a Greek zodiac. The three next cases (78-80) are filled with sepulchral tablets representing various Egyptian divinities, among which the embalmer of the dead, Anubis, ever figures prominently. The cases marked 81, 82, are filled with a collection of rings of ivory, jasper, and cornelian; gold, silver, and porcelain earrings and bracelets; signets with scarabaei, or sacred beetles, in gold, silver, bronze, and some of the Graeco-Egyptian period, in iron; necklaces, ornamented with various religious symbols, in gold, jasper, amethyst; and in the 83rd case are some specimens of old Egyptian glass. The next six cases (84-89) are entirely devoted to sepulchral ornaments, including sepulchral tablets showing priests adoring the sun, scenes of the embalmment of the dead, and devotees adoring their favourite deities; pectoral plates; patches from the network outer coverings of mummies, including the popular scarabaei, wings, sceptres headed with, the lotus flower, and the crowns of upper and lower Egypt, all in porcelain--all taken from the coffins of various mummies. Case 90 contains the coffin of the archon of Thebes, Soter, with the hawk of the sun on the top, and the judgment scenes of the Amenti on the sides. The next three cases (91-93) are filled with more specimens of Egyptian ornaments, including four sides of a sepulchral box in wood (92), and sepulchral tablets. The three cases next in succession (94-96) are filled with amulets of all kinds, chiefly in the form of the scarabaeus, cut in stone. The scarabaeus of the Egyptians was an emblem of the Divinity, which the devout wore about their necks, and hung round the necks of their dead relatives, as in the present day an effigy of the Virgin rests often upon the cold breast of a Catholic corpse. As the visitor will perceive, the collection of amulets comprehends representations of various sacred animals, including the hedgehog. They are, in some cases, nearly four thousand years old. The collection of scarabaei includes one recording the marriage of Amenophis III. to Queen Taia, and several bearing

How to See the British Museum in Four Visits

the name of Rameses, or Sesostris, according to the Greeks. These ornaments are in various substances; the more valuable being in cornelian, and basalt. The following three cases (97-99) contain sepulchral tablets in wood, with various sacred drawings upon them; and in the 100th case are inclosed the sepulchral scarabaei, usually engraved with a prayer, and found inserted in the folds of mummy bandages. Several are costly, as for instance that marked 7875 of green jaspyr, said to have been extracted from the coffin of King Enantef. The next two cases (101, 102) contain various interesting fragments from mummies, including plain scarabaei and other symbolic amulets, and ornaments inscribed with the names of early Egyptian kings. Having noticed these revelations of Egypt's sepulchres, the visitor should turn at once to the eastern wall cases in which he will find a vast collection of

EGYPTIAN DEITIES.

The innumerable little figures scattered throughout the first seven cases are all Egyptian deities with their appropriate symbols, including those in porcelain and stone with holes bored in them for the purpose of attaching them to mummy bandages; those in wood which were carved generally to decorate tombs, and those in bronze which were the household gods. It would be impossible for the general visitor to examine this collection in detail, but he may notice the chief deities with the extraordinary jumble of human and brute life which they present. First of all the visitor will remark, in the first division of the first case, a sandstone figure, seven inches high, seated upon a throne with lotus sceptres, and attendant deities; this is Amenra, the Jupiter of the Egyptians; and in the same case Phtah, the Vulcan of the Egyptians, with a gour, or animal-headed sceptre in both hands, and an oskh, or semi-circular collar, about his neck; the Egyptian Saturn, Sabak, with the head of a crocodile, with the shenti about his loins; and Thoth, the Egyptian Mercury, with an ibis head surmounted by a crescent moon. In the second division, or case, amid the strange figures, the visitor should remark the Egyptian Juno, Mout, or mother, represented in the act of suckling, and wearing the pschent, or cap, worn only by deities and Pharaohs; the Egyptian Minerva, Nepth, on a throne, with the teshr, or inferior cap on her head; a human form with a goat's head, wearing a conical cap ornamented with two ostrich feathers, and disk on goat's horns, representing Num, or water, called Jupiter Chnumis by the Greeks; Khem, the Egyptian Pan, standing on nine bows; a youthful figure with one lock of hair, and supporting the lunar disk, representing Chons, or the Egyptian Hercules; an Egyptian Venus, Athor, in gold, cow-headed; Ra, the sun, seated, and hawk-headed; Nefer Atum, with the lotus flower and plumes for head ornaments, from Memphis, and reverenced as the guardian of the sun's nostril; and the Egyptian Diana, Pasht, or Bubastis, a bronze female figure with the head of a cat. The third division includes a group, in vitrified earth, representing Amenra seated on a feathered throne; a triad, in blue porcelain, of Amoun Mout, the mother, and Chons, or Hercules; a figure in lapis-lazuli of the Egyptian Minerva, Nepth; Num, ram-headed, walking; Ptah-Socharis standing upon two crocodiles, and supporting two hawks on his shoulders; and Pasht, the Egyptian Diana, lion-headed. The third and fourth cases are filled with more specimens of ancient Egyptian deities. In the first division the visitor should remark a stone figure of the Egyptian Pluto, Osiris Pethempamentes, with the atf, or conical cap, on his head, and the curved sceptre, and three-thonged whip in his hand; a figure in stone, seated, wearing a conical cap, and holding the sceptre called a gom, which represents the Egyptian Bacchus, Osiris Ounophris; and a painted wooden figure, kneeling, and supporting a building and a basket, representing the Egyptian Proserpine, Nepththys, mistress of the palace. The second and third divisions contain some remarkable figures, including bronze groups of Osiris-ioh, or the moon, with the lunar disk; a walking figure of Anubis, with a jackal's head; the ibis-headed Thoth, and Har-si-esi with a hawk's head, each pouring a flood of water upon the earth; various hawk-headed and other deities, in the beautiful lapis lazuli, blue porcelain, and green felspar, including Isis suckling her son Horus, and walking with a throne on her head; Nephthys walking; a porcelain Horus with the mystic lock; a blue porcelain plate, representing a procession of female deities; a snake-headed deity, also in blue porcelain; and a porcelain Thoth carrying a scarabaeus. In the fourth division the visitor will at once notice a small monument in calcareous stone, about one foot two inches in height, with various deities represented upon it; also other monuments, one decorated with a flying scarabaeus; Horus seated upon a throne flanked with lions; and Pasht upon a throne supported by two negroes and two Asiatics. The fifth case is devoted also to deities, which the visitor will recognise, and here he should notice the terra-cotta figure, with a buckler and sword, which represents the Mars of the Egyptians, known as Onouris. The principal object in the sixth case is the mummy-shaped coffin of a Theban priest, called Penamen, and grouped near it are offering stands and fragments. The seventh case contains one or two remarkable groups, including some sacred animals; statues of Horns and the son of Horus supporting three vases upon goat's horns; various figures of Khons, one standing on a lotus flower; an extraordinary figure of Phtah-Socharis upon two crocodiles; Ta-ur, an erect hippopotamus, with human breasts, and the back covered by a crocodile's tail; Typhon, ass-headed; and the tortoise-headed guardian of the third hall of the Amenti, recovered from the tombs of the kings at Thebes. Having noticed these remarkable combinations and symbols of the religious idea of ancient Egypt, the visitor should rapidly examine the extraordinary collection of

SACRED ANIMALS,

which exhibit, in their infinite variety, a confusion of species so ingenious and astonishing, that the spectator who has the least zoological enthusiasm is utterly confounded by the strange sights that are here. These animals are collected into four cases (8-11), the two first of which are chiefly devoted to the quadrupeds; and the two last to the birds. Among the former, or quadrupeds, the visitor will particularly remark the cynocephali, or dog-headed baboons, in bronze and stone; various lions; cats, with bored ears; jackals; shrew mice bearing the winged world; bulls; gazelles; a kneeling ibex; a ram walking with the conical cap on its head; a sow with pigs, in bronze; a quadruped with a viper's head; sphinxes, one covered with a lotus; and various models of hares, ram's heads, &c. These animals, that is to say the sacred animals that actually had life, were waited upon by the priests, and the pain of death was inflicted upon any person who killed them. Among the birds are many figures of hawks, some with human faces, others with the solar disk on the head, or the conical cap; the ibis, variously decorated; snakes and fishes; uraei; wooden fragments of vipers; frogs; scorpions; a bronze crocodile; scarabaei, in lapis-lazuli and other substances; emblems of stability; a wooden head of the hippopotamus from the Tombs of the Kings at Thebes; vultures; and snakes.

Next to the cases of sacred animals are two (12, 13) devoted to small statues of various kinds, in various substances. In the first division of these cases are stone heads of priests, and officers of state with long hair; and in the second, many curious objects are arranged, including figures of men seated on thrones; a standing figure of a Pharaoh; a long haired officer of state carved in ebony; rowers, with moveable arms, taken from the models of boats. The third division includes a dark green figure of a royal scribe, kneeling and holding a tablet on which the prenomen of Rameses is visible; kings in various attitudes; the bronze figure of a kneeling priest supporting a bowl containing loaves; an altar of libation, with sacred animals, and vases, cakes, &c.; various figures of scribes and others; a female figure with a calf suspended about the neck by its legs, and the hand resting upon the horns of a gazelle; reclining female figures; parts of two females supporting monkeys; a seated female with blue hair; and fragments of figures. The fourth division contains other Egyptian figures. Having examined these two cases the visitor should approach those in which the larger

EGYPTIAN HOUSEHOLD OBJECTS

and other curiosities are deposited. These cases are six in number (14-19). From these cases the visitor will have an opportunity of gathering a general idea of the domestic comforts of the ancient Egyptians. Here are arranged their chairs, stools, and head-rests, as they were used three thousand years ago. In the first division are, an inlaid stool from Thebes, with a maroon-coloured seat; and a high-backed chair, inlaid with ivory and dark woods, and a seat of cordage, also from Thebes; but the most curious objects in this division are the Egyptian pillows or head-rests, called uls. These are hollowed clumps of wood or metallic substance, supported upon a column, and used by the hardy ancients as rests for the head. In the present day the poorest beggar would think one of these uls a sorry rest for his weary head: yet some of the specimens have the titles of men of distinction engraved upon them. Pillows, however, were not unknown luxuries to the Egyptians, as a pillow of linen, stuffed with water-fowl feathers, and deposited in the second division of the cases under notice, testifies. In this second division are fragments of couches, the decorations chiefly representing animals; fragments, in calcareous stone, from the propylon of the brick pyramid of Dashour; cramps, from Thebes and the temple of Berenice; iron keys from Thebes; bronze hinges; porcelain tiles from the door of a pyramid; an interesting stone model of a house; a model from Upper Egypt of a granary, with a covered shed at one corner from which a man apparently surveyed the operations of the workmen below. A Leghorn mouse, setting aside the feelings of enthusiastic antiquaries

THE EGYPTIAN ROOM

consumed the grain that lay in the model granaries. From this curious relic the visitor will turn with some astonishment to an ancient Egyptian wig: it is curled on the top and plaited at the sides, and is in all respects a well manufactured article. It is a state wig, worn only on great occasions--the Egyptians going habitually closely shaven. In the third division of the cases are assembled various bulky figures, which the visitor will recognise as various Egyptian deities: there is Pasht with his lion's head; Num, ram-headed; Thoth, ibis-headed, and others; also the figure of a Pharaoh, or Egyptian king, with the teshr, a royal cap, all taken from the tombs of the kings at Thebes.

In the two next cases (20, 21) the visitor will find various specimens of the dresses and personal ornaments of the ancient Egyptians. In the first division are a leather cap, cut into net-work from a single piece, the ordinary male head-dress; a leather workman's apron: a palm-leaf basket, and a linen cloth tunic that was found in it at Thebes. The toilet vessels of various substances and shapes, used to contain the metallic dye for the eye-lids, called sthem, worn by the ancient Egyptians, including the cylindrical case, bearing the royal names, are arranged in the second division, together with ivory, porcelain, and other hair studs, and a pair of cord sandals from Memphis. The third division is filled with varieties of Egyptian mirrors, pins, combs, and sandals. The mirrors of the Egyptians consisted of circular metallic plates, with variously ornamented handles. The specimens in this case, which have lost their lustre under centuries of rust, include one with a lotus handle, ornamented with the Egyptian goddess of beauty, Athor; one with a tress of hair as a design for the handle: and others ornamented with the head of the much reverenced hawk. The pins are in bronze and wood, and were used by the Egyptian ladies either to bind the hair or to apply the sthem to the eyelids. The combs show a double row of teeth, and are of wood. The shoes and sandals are of various kinds, but the greatest variety of these articles is deposited in the fourth division of the cases. These are made of palm leaves, wood, and papyrus: those with high-peaked toes are the most ancient, having been worn in the eighteenth dynasty, about fourteen centuries before our era.

The nine following cases (22-32) are devoted to the vases and other domestic vessels of the Egyptians; an intervening case (27) being filled with the cedar coffin of a prophet priest of Amoun in Thebes, elaborately ornamented with various religious symbols. Some of the vases are inscribed with royal names of early dynasties, proving their great antiquity: some of the most elegant dating so far back as fourteen centuries before our era. These specimens of ancient Egyptian workmanship suggest a state of high artistic refinement of a remoter antiquity than the Grecian, wrecks of which lie in the Elgin and other saloons on the basement of the museum. Of the large collection here arranged the visitor will only care to notice the more remarkable specimens. The uses to which these cups and bowls and vases were put, may be inferred partly from their shapes, and partly from the material of which they were made; those of a costly kind being probably the receptacles of the unguents with which the ancient Egyptians of both sexes anointed their persons after the bath; and the larger and less costly varieties being the wine vases, &c, in common use. Two ancient vases are in the first division of the case (22, 23) one with the name of a king before the twelfth dynasty, and the more modern one of the twenty-fifth dynasty. In the second division the visitor should notice the small aragonite vases, resembling wine-glasses; in the third case a slab, upon which are six vases of various shapes in calcareous stone; in the fourth a vase from Lower Egypt, with the quantity it holds inscribed upon it. In the next five cases, 24-27 are filled with cups, and bowls, small vases, and lamps, including pottery vases shaped like the pine cone; blue porcelain vase with a pattern; a highly ornamented porcelain jug; vases in the shape of the hedgehog and the ibis; glass, long-necked vases; a large blue bowl, ornamented with leaves; a porcelain vase of the time of Sesostris, ornamented with petals of the lotus flower; polished terra-cotta vases; double vases; a lamp shaped like a bottle: a vase for libations in terra-cotta, with a spout shaped like a bird's beak; bottle-shaped vase in painted pottery, with three handles, and symbolic decorations; and curious perforated cups on feet. The three cases marked 30-32 contain also some curious vases and lamps, including a vase shaped like a woman playing a guitar, from Thebes; a vase issuing from a flower, in red pottery; a, lamb reclining as a vase; gourd-shaped vases; earthenware bowls covered with various deities; and lamps ornamented with toads, boars' heads, children, and leaves, in relief. Other vases are arranged here and there about the five next cases (33-37) together with agricultural implements; and, strange to say, viands prepared perhaps for some of the mummies that lie in the immediate neighbourhood, together with odd bits and fragments, all illustrative of times before Alexander had bequeathed the Ptolemies to Egypt. In the first two divisions, the remarkable objects are various, bronze buckets with ornamental outlines of various deities and sacred animals; a rectangular bronze table, perforated to receive vessels; bronze lamps, &c.; and in the third division the visitor should certainly notice the two-staged stand of papyrus and cane from a private tomb at Thebes, with trussed ducks and cakes of bread upon it; baskets containing fruits, as figs, pomegranates, dates, cakes of barley, &e. The fourth division contains some old agricultural implements, including the fragments of a sickle found by Belzoni under a statue at Karnak; a wooden pick-axe; an Egyptian hoe; a yoke of acacia wood; eight steps of wood from a rope-ladder, and specimens of palm-fibre rope.

Passing from these interesting relics of ancient manufacturing skill, the visitor will next arrive before two cases (36, 37) of Egyptian fragments of tombs, and weapons of war, illustrating the means of killing and the fashion of burial. In the first division are various goms, or Egyptian sceptres and staffs, some of ebony and some of wood; and the blade of a war-axe, with the name of Thothmes III. inscribed upon it. A variety of offensive weapons are arranged in the second division, including bronze war-axes, one with a hollow silver handle; daggers; bows and arrows, the arrows pointed with triangular bronze heads, and fragments of flint-arrow-heads; fowling-sticks; handsome bronze bladed knives, with agate and other handles, some worked with gold, &c. The fragments in the third division include a knotted rope; a piked club; wooden fan handles; wooden paddles carved with heads of jackals; a mast for the model of a boat; and in the fourth division are a curious cuirass and helmet, from the tombs of Manfaloot, fashioned from a crocodile skin. At this point is another intermediate case containing a mummy, coffin, and boards. The coffin is shaped like a mummy, with a green face, and Netpe, between Isis and Nephthys on the breast, with the deceased being introduced to the deities, among whom he is to be divided by Thoth. This coffin was presented to the Museum by George III.

Having peered into the fragmentary establishments of ancient Egypt, followed the contemporaries of Sesostris into their dining-rooms, even noticed specimens of their dishes, and seen them in their waxen winding-sheets, the visitor may now pass to the next case (39) and notice some of the remains of the materials by the means of which they recorded their actions, and traced their lineaments. Here are displayed the ancient Egyptian pens and pencils, colours and ink, all shrivelled and discoloured with the mould of centuries, but remaining still to bear witness to the early love of knowledge and of art, that urged the Egyptian scribe and the Egyptian artist to fashion them. In the first division are the rectangular pallets, with grooves for the wooden pens or reeds, and hollows for the colour or ink; and here, too, are the kash, or pens used by the ancient scribes. The pallets have inscriptions upon them; on one there is an invocation to the goddess of writing. Fragments of one or two colours, with the palm-leaf baskets in which they were deposited are also in this case; together with stands with small colour vases; slabs with colour jars; mullets for grinding, a basket with paint-brushes made of palm-fibres; and upon a thin piece of cedar wood is a portrait of an Egyptian female of the Greek period. Amidst other minute objects lie Egyptian folding wax tablets for writing; a cylindrical ink-box, with a chain attached to hold the pen case; seals of various kinds with impressions of bulls, jackals, and hieroglyphics; portion of a calendar on stone; and fragments of Egyptian writing on stone, and chiefly from tombs. These fragments illustrative of the Egyptian character are continued in the first two divisions of the cases marked 40, 41, including a panel and stud from an ebony box inscribed with the titles of Amenophis III. and his daughter; and a fragment in ebony, with an inscribed dedication to Anubis. Among the miscellaneous objects also in these divisions are various boxes in wood, papyrus, one veneered with white and red ivory, some inscribed with names; and one with a pyramidal cover, veneered with ivory and ornamented with figures and birds. The next or third division is filled with varieties of Egyptian spoons. Some of these are curious. They are chiefly of wood; but some are of ivory. Among them are wooden spoons, shovel, egg and cartouche-shaped; one with the handle carved in the shape of lotus flowers; one with a moveable cover from Memphis; one with the handle representing a gazelle, and within fish demolishing a water plant, from Thebes; one in the shape of a fish; one circular, with a lotus handle and a hawk cynocephalus on its edge; one with the form of a fish for a bowl, and a fox seizing the fish for a handle; and others equally curious in point of design. The last, or fourth division of the case is full of ancient Egyptian building materials, including fragments of painted plaster; stamps for bricks; palm-fibre brushes for colouring walls, and smoothing tools.

EGYPTIAN TOOLS

are disposed through the two cases (42, 43) which the visitor should now examine. In the first division are some palm-leaf baskets; wooden mallets, one found in the masonry of the great pyramid at Abooseir; and staves; in the second division a large variety of curious tools is exhibited, including Egyptian saws, bradawls, chisels, an adze, axe blades, knives of bronze, generally inscribed with hieroglyphics, hones, bronze nails; mysterious bronze tools, the use of which is unknown, all interesting to those who are in any way interested in the history of the wonderful people who inhabited the valley of the Nile, and wielded these tools there, when our island was an untilled desert. The third division of the case contains strange handles decorated with the popular lotus flower, fragments of an ivory gorget, with figures of various animals oddly grouped upon it; various fragments of carving, and pedestals bearing inscriptions; and in the fourth, or last, division of the case are various baskets, coloured and plain. The first division of the next case (44, 45) is also given up to palm-leaf baskets of various descriptions, which the visitor should examine as illustrating the perfection to which the workers of the palm-leaf brought their handicraft. Leaving the tools and baskets behind, the visitor will now approach the

EGYPTIAN MUSICAL INSTRUMENTS,

which occupy the second division of the case. It is well known that music was generally cultivated by the ancient Egyptians, even before Terpander had devised a system of musical notation: and that in their religious ceremonies music was much used. The sistrum, of which the visitor will notice one or two samples in the division, was the instrument most generally used. It consisted of wires suspended through the sides of an arch, to which a handle, generally highly ornamented with the head of Athor, as in the one in the case, is fixed:--the wires terminating with heads of sacred animals, upon which rings were suspended that produced sounds by being shaken backwards and forwards.

There are also some Egyptian harps; portions of flutes found in the northern brick pyramids at Dashour; a pipe with seven burnt holes in it; and a pair of bronze cymbals tied together by a band of linen. The division next to that in which the musical instruments are arranged, is filled with

EGYPTIAN TOYS.

Perhaps, no portion of this interesting Egyptian room so forcibly impresses the spectator with the truth and reality of its revelations, as these rude toys, that must have been handled by prattling Egyptian children, when all was dark throughout

Europe, save on the shore of the southern sea, where glimmered fitful lights of awakening civilisation, and Homer was enshrining the poor knowledge of his period in the splendid fancies of his poet soul. Not vastly different from the rude dolls of the present century must these of Egypt have been when fresh from the workman's hand. They are in a very disabled state now, however; one being a rude representation of an Egyptian Miss Biffen, altogether guiltless of legs; and others, the flat variety, having hair made of clay beads. In the case with these relics are porcelain models of eggs, balls, fruit; wooden fish; leather and palm-leaf balls, stuffed; dice, and various draughtsmen, with the heads of cats; and one with the figure of a jackal. The last two divisions of the case under notice are entirely filled with a variety of specimens of

ANCIENT EGYPTIAN FABRICS.

This division is always interesting to visitors who have any knowledge of the essential excellences of textile fabrics. There can be no doubt of the high repute in which the linens of ancient Egypt were held of old; but the samples which have remained in a state of preservation up to the present day, being mostly bandages of the coarse cloths from mummies, it is hardly possible to estimate fairly the excellence of the fabrics with which, the great men of ancient Egypt adorned their persons and those of their wives. However, one or two samples of linen, as fine as the celebrated muslins of India, remain, and the visitor should notice particularly those clothes in the case with fine blue selvage. In the case also are part of the bandages of an Egyptian mummy of the Greek period, and a sample of ancient Egyptian linen bleached by the modern process. With these specimens are skeins of thread, spindles, and knitting-needles; bronze sewing needles; and a hackle for flax-dressing. With this case the visitor closes his examination of the wall cases of the Egyptian room. On taking a general survey of the room, the objects that will first attract his attention are the casts of the remarkable sculptures from the entrance to the temple at Beit-onally near Kalabshe, placed over the wall-cases against the eastern and western walls. These are faithful representations of the painted sculpture for which the ancient Egyptians were famous, about thirteen centuries before our era. The specimens in the room represent the triumphs of the second Rameses. The cast against the eastern wall is in two distinct compartments. In the first, Rameses, accompanied by his sons, is driving his vanquished Ethiopian enemies into a wood:

in the second part the conqueror is investing the vanquished Ethiopian prince with a gold chain, and behind are the spoils of war, and Ethiopians leading strange oxen to the victor; while, in the lower division, the vanquished prince is presenting a load of tributary treasure to the king, followed by a crowd of Ethiopians, leading all kinds of animals. These paintings, as the visitor will observe, are painted without regard to light and shade, the figures are huddled together, and the drawing is of the most rigid description. The casts against the western wall are in five compartments, and celebrate the victories of Rameses over the Asiatic nations. In the first compartment Rameses is receiving his Asiatic captives; in the second he is about to decapitate a prisoner; in the third, in his kingly cap, he is defeating an Asiatic army, who are represented in active flight; in the fourth he is attacking an Asiatic fortress; and in the fifth the king is again receiving Asiatic prisoners. Having noticed these remarkable antiquities, the visitor should examine the plaster models, placed upon the central table of the room, of the obelisks of Karnak and Heliopolis. Above the door is a leather cross, from the dress of a Copt priest, supposed to be about twelve hundred years old. Above various cases are placed mummy coffins, and figures of deities too large for the cases; but the mummy-case deposited over case 31 is worth special attention. It is scooped out of the trunk of a tree, has the face painted black, a vulture on the chest, and other ornaments and symbols. Near it, over cases 30-32, are deposited four sepulchral vases of a military officer, containing the parts removed from the body in the process of embalming. Each vase was sacred to a deity; the first, containing the stomach and appendages, was sacred to Amset the first genius of the dead; the second, containing the lesser intestines, was presided over by the second genius of the dead, Hapi; the lungs and heart, deposited in the third vase, were sacred to Siumutf, the third genius; and to the fourth genius the vase containing the liver and gall-bladder was dedicated.

    The visitor having noticed these objects has done with the Egyptian room. It is well, however, to pause upon the threshold, and before dismissing these interesting glimpses into the life, long since scattered as dust, upon the soil of Egypt, to call to mind the prominent points of the impressive story that may be read in the room he is about to quit. He may wander back through the histories of ages upon ages; pause before the revelations of Herodotus; and recall the mighty romances of Homer; and, pausing even there, where all is so dim, and little understood, turn once more to these fragmentary monuments of a civilisation that existed even centuries before the great Greek poet. So silently, for us of the present hour, time rolled by in those days, that we fail to grasp the measure of the distance which separates our fret and toil of the nineteenth century, from that busy valley of the Nile; when the second Rameses reigned in all his glory; when precise artists were ruling geometrical lines upon stones to make their careful drawings; and painters, with their palm-fibre brushes, all unconscious of the critics that lay yet silently in the womb of time, who would shovel the dust and dirt of centuries from before their works, and tell the story of Rameses from these rude revelations. Curious thoughts crowd in every busy brain, before these strange relics. Lost in the depths of the past, the mind, with a leap, often grasps at the future; and men will be found seriously saying to themselves, as they notice how we depend for our knowledge of ancient Egyptian fabrics upon the shrouds of ancient Egyptians,--what, if we looked forward, and in the remote centuries that are rolling toward us, see all our vast and busy Lancashire some layers underground, and archaeologists busy with our winding sheet! Well, at the least, these thoughts are not idle. It does all of us good to think often of what has been, and to dream of the future to which we are driving "down the ringing grooves of time"--to think sometimes of the fine people who had their glorious days, when London was distributed, untouched by human hands, in clayey strata, and remote stone quarries; and hereabouts, to the minds of the Greeks, lay the islands of the blessed.

The visitor should now proceed southward into the room called The Bronze Room. Here are collected the ancient bronzes of which the Museum trustees are in possession; including specimens of the fine castings of ancient Greece, which, with all our modern contrivances, we cannot surpass in the present day. The cases to the left are filled with a supplementary collection of the remains of ancient Egyptian art, for which space could not be found in the Egyptian room. These occupy no less than twenty-six cases. The first eleven cases (1-11) are filled with various sepulchral fragments in various substances, and porcelain and terra-cotta figures, which the visitor who has just emerged from the Egyptian room will again recognise. Here the strange figures of the Egyptian deities occur again and again; but the visitor should pause before the case 10, 11, in which are deposited models of the Egyptian funeral boats, in stone and wood, from Thebes, and on the fourth shelf a Roman caricature on papyrus, representing lions and goats playing at dice, and foxes driving geese. In the Egyptian cases are more specimens of cynocephali, jackal, and hawks' heads, models of the four sepulchral vases, in pottery and wood; more mummy coffins, fragments of inscribed pottery, large Egyptian terra-cotta vases, and in cases 24, 25, are deposited some fragments in terra-cotta, and bronze excavated by Mr. Layard, in ancient Assyria. Having glanced at these Egyptian cases the visitor should turn at once to the collection of

GREEK AND ROMAN BRONZES,

which fill the cases numbered from 29 to 112. The visitor particularly interested in Greek and Roman art, might here spend an entire day. Bronze, a mixture of copper and tin, was used by the ancients for the manufacture of all kinds of edge-tools, long before iron was smelted from the earth in which it is invariably found; and mineralogists of the present day are surprised to see the works which the ancients executed with a material, that no modern workmen could use as a cutting medium. Stone masons' chisels, and fine edged weapons of war, were made of bronze in those days. The collection of bronzes which the visitor is now about to examine, cannot be said to be a perfect collection; yet it contains some beautiful specimens, and one that is said to be the finest bronze in Europe. The antiquarian pauses with delight before these marvellous specimens of ancient skill; and reflecting upon the difficulties which beset the caster in bronze, it is astonishing to see the precision and the exquisite finish with which the artists of ancient Greece and Rome performed their labours. Some of their bronze manufacture were hammered, but most of those works from which we derive a knowledge of their greatness as artists were cast. Of those colossal bronzes which were studded about Rome, Athens, and Delphos, few remain at the present day. The material of which they were composed was too valuable to escape the clutch of barbaric conquerors; therefore the bronzes which remain are chiefly of a small size, but still sufficiently perfect to assure us of the great works that filled every open place in the towns of ancient Greece and Rome. In these cases the visitor will find a great number of bronze utensils and personal ornaments: metal mirrors; lamps; incense vessels, or thuribula; the saucers for pouring libations, called paterae; tripods of all kinds and variously ornamented; candelabra; and the clasps of the Romans called fibulae.

Beginning with the first case, 29, 30, the visitor will first remark three ancient vases or amphorae, and five jugs, from Corfu, aged about five centuries before our era; and in the same cases, on the third and fourth shelves, Athenian vases, variously ornamented with geometrical designs, animals, and birds, in the most ancient style. The next case also contains vases of the most ancient style, from Athens, including a fine specimen surmounted by two horses. In cases 33, 34, are further specimens of the vases of ancient Greece, on some of which red figures are traced upon a black ground, and on others a red ground is adopted, with the ornamental figures in black: among the ornaments on those vases the visitor should notice the cupids represented in blue and white on one of these vases, and on another the figure of a crawling boy, with a low stool and an apple before him. The vases in the next cases (35, 36) contain some fine specimens of Athenian art about the time of Pericles, with figures traced red and black, representing Orestes and Electra at the tomb of Agamemnon. In these cases also are some Athenian glass vases, and opaque glass vessels from Melos; terra-cotta bas-reliefs, representing Bellerophon destroying the Chimera; Perseus destroying the gorgon Medusa, and other classical subjects; and upon the third shelf, amid unguent boxes, terra-cotta lamps, and a terra-cotta doll, is a curious vase containing bones, with a silver Athenian coin, attached to the jar by careful relatives, to pay for the deceased's transit across the Styx. A collection of terra-cotta figures are arranged upon the four shelves of case 37. These include an ancient comic actor as Hercules; Athenian ladies bearing water jugs, called Hydriophorae; Ceres; a dancing group from Athens; animals; stools; and dancing figures from the south of Italy. No less than three hundred and thirty-three handles from the wine vessels or amphorae of ancient Rhodes are deposited in cases 38, 39. Some are inscribed with the names of the chief magistrate. Varieties of vessels in terra-cotta fill the two first shelves of the cases 40, 41, from Etruria; upon the third shelf are fragments of large bronzes, including the staff of AEsculapius with the serpent; and the bronze groups distributed upon the fourth shelf include three figures of Hercules; and two figures supposed to be a Ptolemy and his queen arrayed as Fortune. The cases 42-45 are filled with bronze weapons, including spear-heads from the sepulchres of Etruria; arrow-heads and bronze swords of the Roman time; standards with the famous Roman eagles; helmets, including a famous one dedicated to Jupiter Olympius, by Hiero I. on the occasion of gaining a victory over the Tuscans at Cumae, upwards of four centuries before our era; and one found at Olympia, dedicated by the Argives; bronze plates, and military belts, from Vulci. The next six cases (46-51) are filled with various Grecian and Roman antiquities, of which the visitor should particularly notice amid bronze amphorae, tripods, glass beads, weights in the shape of busts, sacrificial knives, and bronze hatchet heads, three cistae or boxes, with classical groups in relief upon them, the subject of one being Hercules grasping serpents. These cistae were the toilette boxes of the ancients. Here too the visitor should remark the hearth (a tripod) with charcoal still upon it, with fire-irons and cooking utensils; and a variety of tripods variously ornamented with sphinxes, Boreas carrying away Orithyia; and leaden vases from Delos, holding the ashes of the dead. An interesting collection of candelabra, from the Etruscan sepulchres, is arranged in the next cases (52, 53). These candelabra were highly esteemed throughout ancient Greece. They are decorated chiefly with mythological subjects, and have, attached to them, vessels for dipping into larger vessels. Those in the next case (54) are of the Roman period. Having glanced at the censers and bronze lamps in the next cases (56-57) the visitor may pass on to the case numbered 58-64, in which is a large collection of bronze vessels, including unguent vases, which are the most highly decorated, braziers, cauldrons, and jugs. The two next cases contain a great number of bronze figures of various heathen deities, representations of mythological events. Here are, a winged Victory holding an egg; figures of Juno Sospita; figures for mirrors; Apollos; a giant hurling a rock; one of the Gorgons; figures of Mars, in the old grotesque style; a reclining Dionysus, drinking; satyrs; Aphrodite; Aurora bearing off Tithonus or Cephalus; Hercules; Ariadne playing on the lyre; Hercules killing the Maenalian stag; Minerva; and other figures, all drawn from Grecian mythology. These cases present, at a glance, more than any other in the collection, the various excellences of ancient bronzes. The ancient mirrors are arranged in the next two cases (68, 69)--one polished to show their old effect; and in the 70th case are Etruscan and Roman fibulae or clasps in general use in the olden time, in lieu of buttons or hooks. The drainings of the lake of Monte Falterona brought to light the most attractive objects of the next three cases (71-73), including the fine Etruscan statue of Mars, the large statue of a youth; and here also are a group of Aurora bearing off Memnon; and a satyr and a bacchante for the top of a candelabrum. Finely ornamented mirrors, with figures chased, bas-relief, representing, among other subjects, Minerva before Paris; Achilles arming before Thetis; a winged Hercules killing the Lernean Hydra; Juno and her rivals preparing for the judgment of Paris; Hercules bearing off a female figure; Venus holding a dove, as a mirror handle; the Dioscuri, Clytemnestra and Helen; Aphrodite nursing Eros; and Dolon, Ulysses, and Diomed. Bronze figures of Greek and Roman divinities fill the next case, including a silver group of Saturn devouring his children; no less than nineteen Jupiters, one in silver with a goat at his side. These are continued in the following case (78), including Isis; Ganymede and the eagle; Terpsichore; Apollos; Junos; a fine Apollo from Paramythia; a Triton, with crab's claws, and a face turning into sea weed; Dianas, one, in silver, holding a crescent; and Neptune, distinguishable by his trident. Three cases, next in order of number (80-82), are devoted to ancient Roman horse-trappings. Busts of Minerva occupy the most prominent positions in the 83rd case; and in the next case (84) are no less than twenty-one figures of Mercury, one of which, distinguishable by the gold collar about the neck, is reputed the most beautiful bronze in Europe. These figures of Mercury are in various attitudes. Here the cocks, emblematic of the athletic games, are before him--there he is flying on Jupiter's eagle; and near these figures are arranged twenty-eight figures of Venus; in one place the goddess is rising from the sea, in another she is arranging her sandal, or riding her swan. Playful Cupids, thirty-five in number, and gambolling variously, occupy the position next in order to the figures of Venus. Here the little god is running, there he bears the anointing-box of Venus--there he is laughing, in another corner his laughter is turned to tears, and in another he is ingloriously intoxicated. In another direction he is exhibited in his amiable moods, feeding a hare with grapes, or toying with a swan. The next case (86) contains an assortment of ancient glazed articles including glass studs, buttons, &c., from the sepulchres of Etruria; bronze sandals from Armentum; and glazed ware of various shapes. In the 87th case are deposited four curious fragments from Perugia, of chariot chasings, representing various warlike emblems and doings; and an ancient scabbard engraved with an outline of Briseis led by Achilles. Deities fill the next case (89), including fourteen figures of Harpocrates; a Pan; and figures of Bacchus. Silenus, with silver eyes and a crown set with garnets, will be found in the next case (90) where Hercules is strangling the Nemean lion; and another Silenus kneeling on a wine-skin. Cupid is seizing the weapons of the strong Hercules while the latter sleeps; in the next case (91), here also he is grappling with the Maenalian stag, and Pan shows his goat's legs. The 92nd, 93rd and 94th cases are filled with various mirrors from Athens; the anciently prized knuckle bones of a small animal; bronze earrings from a tomb in Cephalonia; sling bullets found at Saguntum; part of a lyre, and wooden flutes discovered near Athens; a gilt myrtle crown; glass mosaics from the Parthenon; iron knives and fetters from Athens; a jar that once held the famed Lycian eye ointment; one of the bronze tickets of a judge; and leaden weights. Hercules is vigorously at work in the groups of the next case (95), and herein are figures of Victory and Fortune; two sphinxes, and other groups. The head of Polyphemus appears prominently in the 96th case; and in the remaining cases miscellaneously grouped, are ancient dice, some of which have been loaded, suggesting the antiquity of roguery; ivory hair pins; bronze needles; glass beads; fragments of cornelian and other cups, and glass; bronze figures of animals; inlaid and enamel work; styli for writing upon wax; ancient medical instruments; and old Roman finger-rings.

Over the Egyptian cases are deposited fac-similes of paintings of a tomb at Vulci, discovered in the year 1832. These represent various ancient games of racing and leaping. Over the cases 38-58 are other fac-similes from a tomb, also at Vulci, in a mutilated condition; and against the southern wall are the ceilings of the tomb. Having examined these things the visitor should proceed on his southward course, and, passing through the southern entrance of the bronze room, enter the fine apartment, known as the Etruscan room, in which the

ETRUSCAN VASES

are arranged. These are a series of earthen vases discovered in Italy. These painted vases are the spoil from the tombs of the ancient Etruscans. The Etruscans inhabited the northern parts of Italy, and flourished there in a state of comparative civilisation, when the rest of the Peninsula, save where the Greeks were busy on its southern shore, was in a barbarous state. The Etruscan tombs present various degrees of ornament according to the wealth of their occupant, but in all of them painted vases of some description are found. It is maintained by many learned men that these beautiful vases were not a native manufacture, but were bought by the Etruscans of the Greeks of Southern Italy, who imported them from the famous potteries of Athens. The Greek inscriptions on some of these vases, and the Greek subjects from which the decorations are taken, tend strongly to confirm this hypothesis. It is, however, altogether a mystery why the Etruscans surrounded their dead with these vases. They were not used to hold human bones, nor to contain food for the deceased; but that the Etruscans held them in high estimation as sepulchral ornaments is certain from the fact that they are found universally in their tombs, the finer and more elaborate in the sepulchres of the rich, and the coarser and plainer kinds in the graves of the poor. The visitor will do well to walk carefully round this room in which the Etruscan vases belonging to the Museum are deposited. They are arranged in the supposed chronological order in which they were manufactured; the clumsy and coarse ware being placed in the first case, as exhibiting the dawn of the potter's art, and the more elaborate and highly-wrought specimens being arranged in regular order of improvement in the succeeding cases.

The first five cases are filled with clumsy black ware, ornamented in some cases with figures in relief, and extracted from tombs discovered on the site of the oldest Etruscan towns, which circumstance has led antiquaries to allow the Etruscans the honour of having fashioned these rude specimens of pottery; but as the samples display a higher degree of skill they refuse to allow the Etruscans the merit of having improved the clumsiness of their early handiwork. In the sixth and seventh cases are pale vases with deep red figures, chiefly of animals upon them, chiefly from Canino and Vulci. The exertions of the Prince of Canino in excavating on his estate in search of Etruscan tombs and their treasures are well known; and the enthusiasm with which Sir William Hamilton, while on his embassy at Naples, bought the curiosities of Etruscan tombs, should be remembered. Few Englishmen, however, can think pleasantly of those times when the Hamiltons were at Naples, when Lady Hamilton did her country great services; then recall the picture of the poor woman fed by a charitable neighbour at Calais, think of Horatio's last words, and then of the country that forgets the woman's service, and the hero's dying words. Well, the visitor may pass on his way amidst these spoils from Etruscan tombs, and forgetting the family to whom we owe many of them, serenely watch the gradual improvement in the manufacture. The best have black figures upon a dark ground. The glass cases in the centre of the room contain those vases which are painted on both sides. On the walls of the room above the cases are fac-similes of paintings from some of the Etruscan tombs. Some of them represent dances and games; but one represents a female in the act of covering the head of a man who has just expired, while a male figure is drawing a covering over the feet, and two spectators are in attitudes of grief in the neighbourhood. Having roamed amid the spoils of Etruscan tombs, the search after which is now a settled business in parts of Italy, the visitor may take a southerly direction through two empty rooms into that at the southern extremity of the western wing. Here a few miscellaneous objects are deposited, amongst which in the eastern cases he should notice some curious old enamels, and the frescoes from St. Stephen's Chapel, Westminster, and on the floor, a model of the Victory. He should then turn in an easternly direction into the Ethnographical room, which, to the visitor without a guide has very much the appearance of a confined curiosity shop; but on inspection proves to be an interesting compartment of the Museum, in which curiosities illustrative of the civilisation of various countries and continents are arranged. Before applying himself to the wall cases, however, the visitor would do well to advance to the eastern extremity of the room, noticing the objects deposited in the central space by the way. These consist of Flaxman's cast of the shield of Achilles; a model of the Thugs fashioned at Madras by a native artist; a model of a moveable temple; her Majesty's present to the museum of a great Chinese bell, surmounted by the Chinese national dragon, and decorated with figures of Buddh, from a temple near Ningpo; and various cromlechs or sepulchres of the ancient Britons, ruder in their construction than those with which the visitor has lately busied himself. Having arrived at the eastern end of the room, the visitor should advance to the northern wall cases, and begin his inspection. He will at once remark that the first five cases (1-5) are devoted to

CHINESE CURIOSITIES.

These are distributed with particular regard to the economy of space, and accordingly the visitor may see at a glance objects huddled together, the uses of which are of the most opposite nature. On the first shelf of cases 1, 2, are distributed the tally of a Chinese soldier describing his age and place of residence; ladies' gloves; military boots; bows and arrows; and the mock spears shown above the walls of Woosang in 1842 to intimidate the British forces. The second shelf exhibits the grotesque varieties of Chinese deities and leaders of sects; and in other parts of the cases are endless Chinese curiosities, including Chinese scales and weights; padlocks; mirrors; a pair of Chinese spectacles in a leather case; shoe brushes from Shanghai; chopsticks; a brass pipe; Chinese mariners' compasses; a Chinese bank-note, value one dollar; Chinese needles; agricultural implements; joss sticks; the sea-weed eaten by the Chinese; ancient bronze bell; vase in shape of a lotus leaf; and an advertisement for quack pills. The visitor should remark the great royal wicker shield that is on the top of the case, ornamented with the head of a tiger; and the model of a junk. The third case contains Chinese divinities, of which the goddess of Mercy, Kwan-yin, on the first shelf, is the most noticeable figure. The two last cases 4 and 5 given up to Chinese, are filled chiefly with Chinese musical instruments, including the pair of sticks used by Chinese beggars as castanets to attract attention to their petitions; Chinese shuttlecocks, made of feathers and lead, the Chinese battledores being the soles of their feet, suggestive of vigorous exercise; fly-flaps; surgical instruments; paints; boxes; and Japanese shoes. Over these cases is a circular stand, in twenty-two parts, representing, in relief, the chief deities of the Hindoo mythology. The four next cases (6-9) are given up to

INDIAN CURIOSITIES.

Among the miscellaneous collection of objects crowded into these four cases are many figures of Buddha in earthenware, wood, alabaster and ivory; bronze divinities of the Hindoo Pantheon; Hindoo playing cards; copper-plates containing grants of land; a Hindoo mathematical instrument; a powder-horn from Burtpoor; Affghan cloak and pistol; bows and arrows; baggage and accommodation boats; and early Arabian bronze water ewers inlaid with silver. Over the Indian cases are figures of Hindoo deities, including a bronze figure of Siva with four arms, and Lakshmi, the wife of Vishnu. The four following cases (10-13) are chiefly filled with

AFRICAN CURIOSITIES

of a miscellaneous description, and from various parts of the continent. These include, in cases 10, 11, Nubian and Abyssinian baskets; Arabic quadrants; Egyptian water-bottles; sandals, and a variety of other manufactures from Ashantee, including a shuttle, and specimens of native cotton cloth; an iron bar used as a medium of exchange, and worth about one shilling on the African coast; gourd boxes and calabashes; cloths and other curiosities collected on the Niger Expedition; specimens of native silk from Egga; a skin bottle for holding galena to colour the eyelids; opaque glass beads from Abyssinia; all kinds of arms from French Guiana, Fernando Po, Abyssinia, and Nubia, including a Nubian spear, enveloped with a snake's skin from Thebes. Over the cases an Ashantee loom for weaving narrow cloth, and Abyssinian baskets, and at the side an Indian inlaid cabinet. Passing from these cases, the visitor at once reaches those devoted to

AMERICAN CURIOSITIES.

The cases numbered from 14-21 are filled with articles illustrative of the life and climate of the Esquimaux, and the extreme northern regions of America, including the native fishing-hooks and lines; models of canoes; skin dresses, men's boots from Kotzebue's Sound; Lapland trousers; utensils made of the horn of the musk ox; Esquimaux woman's hair ornaments; over the cases hereabouts the sledge which Sir E. Parry brought from Baffin's Bay, and a canoe from Behring's Straits; waterproof fishing jackets, made from the intestines of the whale; harpoons of bone tipped with meteoric iron; specimens of rude sculpture from these northern regions; clubs; hatchets; the magic dome of an Iceland witch; baskets and mats; calumets of peace; scalps; a model of a cradle, showing the method adopted by the Indians of the Columbia River to flatten their children's heads. The cases 23, 24, are filled with curiosities from more southerly parts of the North American continent; and chiefly with various objects from the most interesting of the old inhabitants of America--the Mexicans. The collection from Mexico, including their divinities, specimens of their arts, &c., are arranged in seven cases (24-30). The objects from Guiana occupy the greater part of cases 31-34; and the remarkable objects in the 35th case are the dried body of a female, from New Granada; a mummy from New Granada wrapped in cotton cloths; a curious Peruvian mummy of a child, the legs curiously bound up; and silver and gold Peruvian sepulchral ornaments. The cases marked 36, 37, are devoted to objects from South America, including black earthern vessels from cemeteries in Peru; bows and poisoned arrows; and a sacrificial bason, ornamented with serpents, supposed to be one from the temple of the Sun at Cuzco. The rest of the cases contain miscellaneous objects from groups of islands. The contributions from the Marquesas and Sandwich Islands are in cases 53-56; the war dresses, of feathers, &c., from Tahiti, in case 57; and the nets and baskets, clubs and tatooing instruments from the Friendly Islands will be found arranged in cases 65, 66. On the second shelf of cases 66, 67, is deposited a tortoise-shell bonnet, made in imitation of an European bonnet from Navigator's Island. Cases 68, 69, are devoted to objects from New Zealand; and those marked 70, 71, were collected during an exploring expedition into Central Australia. The last cases are devoted to miscellaneous objects from the Fiji Islands, Borneo, and other localities; and with these the visitor should close his second visit to the Museum; regaining the ante-room to the Southern Zoological gallery, by passing out of the Ethnographical room through its eastern opening. He has now completed the examination of the galleries of the Museum with the exception of the print and medal rooms, which are not open to the public generally, but are reserved for the use of artists and antiquarians. He has dipped into many sciences on his two journeys; made some acquaintance with the history of the animals that frequent the different parts of the world; dwelt amid the fossil fragments of long ages past; examined the elementary substances of which the earth's crust is composed; been with the dust of men that lived before Jerusalem was made for ever memorable; surveyed the spoils of Etruscan tombs; and lingered amid the varieties of household things from the barbarous nations of the present hour; and not wholly profitless have the journeys been, even if the scientific mysticism be not mastered, so that there remains in the mind a general impression of the time that has gone by, the great laws that govern the universe, and the humility that becomes man, when he sees his individuality, in relation with the mighty past, and the great progresses of Nature.

END OF THE SECOND VISIT.

VISIT THE THIRD.

The visitor, on entering the British Museum for the third time, will commence his examination of the massive Antiquities, which are scattered throughout the noble galleries that stretch along the western basement of the building. His spirit must again wander to the remote past. Again must he recur to the ancient civilisation of southern Europe, and the busy people that covered the valley of the Nile before Alexander breathed. He has already examined the household utensils, the bodies, the ornaments, and the food of the ancient Egyptians, and has had more than a glimpse of the artistic excellence to which they attained long before our Christian era. Of the sepulchral caves of Thebes, of the massive pyramids sacred to the ancient Pharaohs, of the strange images of beasts and men, of the sacred beetles, and the universal Ibis, he has already examined minute specimens arranged in the cases of the Egyptian Room; but he has yet to witness those evidences of power, and scorn of difficulties, exhibited in the colossal works of the Egyptian people.

On entering the Museum for the third time, the visitor should turn to the left, and passing under the staircase, enter the galleries devoted to Ancient Sculpture. He will at once be struck with the strange allegorical figures clustered on all sides, the broken bodies, the fragments of arms and legs, the corners of slabs, and other dilapidations. Here a fine figure is without a nose, there Theseus holds aloft two handless arms, and legs without feet. The visitor who has not the least insight into the heart of all these collections of fragments from tombs, and temples, and neglected ruins, is perhaps inclined to laugh at the enthusiasm with which they are generally examined, and the rapturous strains in which the greatest critics have written of them. Not to all people is the enthusiasm of Lord Elgin comprehensible. Why not allow the fragments of the Parthenon to be ground into fine white mortar, and the busts of ancient heroes to be targets for the weapons of Turkish youths? are questions which a few utilitarians may be inclined to ask; and it would certainly be difficult to show, for instance in figures, the gain the country has made by expending 35,000L. on the Elgin marbles: in the same way that it is difficult to appraise the beneficial influence of beauty, or to test the developments of the universe by double entry.

But let the visitor pace these noble galleries of his national museum with a reverent heart, let him learn from these beautiful labours of long ago, that not only to him and his fellows of the proud nineteenth century, when fiery words are flashing through the seas, and steam fights like a demon with time, were the living years pregnant with the glories of art; but that the Egyptian, with his rude bronze chisel, cut his native rocks with no unskilful hand, before the Son of God lay cradled in a manger.

Past the bewildering fragments of art in the south-western gallery to the south-western corner of the building, then south like an arrow to the northern end of the sculpture rooms, should the visitor at once proceed. He will pass by fragments of Assyrian, Greek, and Roman art, but to these he should now pay little heed, as his immediate business is with the fine gallery of

EGYPTIAN SCULPTURE,

which is the most northernly apartment or gallery of the western wing. Here he will at once notice the rows of Sarcophagi, which are ranged on either side of the central passage of the gallery. These colossal outer-coffins contained the mummies of distinguished Egyptians. Along the walls of the room are ranged the sepulchral tablets, or tombstones of ancient Egyptians, and the inscriptions generally record the name and age of a deceased person; and in some cases, points of domestic history and pious sentences. Their dates range over a space of time amounting to more than twenty centuries. Interspersed with these are other sculptures, chiefly of Egyptian deities; but the attention of the visitor will be probably attracted first to the

EGYPTIAN OUTER COFFINS.

The visitor, having reached the northern end of the Egyptian Saloon, should turn to the south, and begin a minute examination of its contents. The sarcophagi, or outer coffins of stone, in which the rich ancient Egyptians deposited the embalmed bodies of their relations, occupy the greater part of the ground space of the saloon. They are massive shells, hewn from the solid rock, polished and engraved skilfully with hieroglyphics, which, so far as the learned have been able to decipher, record the exploits of the great men they contained. Some of them are in the shape of common boxes with raised lids; while in others, attempts to represent the features of the deceased, and a rough outline of a mummy are apparent. These massive coffins, which are upwards of three thousand years old, and are eloquent with the mystic written language of that remote antiquity, deserve more than a transient notice even from the unscientific visitor. Mummies were found in most of these, proving their use. Some were discovered placed in an erect, and others in a recumbent posture, in the tombs of Thebes, or on the sites of ancient cities.

Of the sarcophagi or coffins, fashioned in the shape of a mummy, the visitor should notice that in calcareous stone, numbered 47, which was discovered at Tana; another, with the paintings restored, marked 39; another in green basalt, marked 33, known to be that of a female called Auch, decorated with the embalming deities, and inscribed with a prayer on behalf of the deceased woman; and one of later date which has held the remains of a member of the priestly class, numbered 17. To arrive at a fair estimate of the average art displayed in these ancient sepulchral remains, it is worth the trouble of the visitor to wander a little about the saloon from one specimen to the next immediately connected with, or proximately resembling it. Having examined the coffins shaped like mummies, the visitor should next direct his attention to the massive oblong cases which lie upon the ground on either side of him.

The first of these which he may examine is that marked 32. This sarcophagus was excavated from the back of the palace of Sesostris, near Thebes. Athor appears in bas-relief upon the lid; the sun is represented in the interior, together with Heaven represented as a female, and a repetition of the goddess Athor.

The names of several royal ladies have been deciphered from the inscriptions, which are the addresses of deities. The black granite chest of a sarcophagus, numbered 23, is that of a royal scribe named Hapimen. Here the well-known figures of the Amenti, the embalmer Anubis, and other deities and symbols, will remind the visitor of the Egyptian room up stairs, with its strange green little images of figures half human and half bestial. Round the interior are the deities to whom the various parts of the human body were severally dedicated. Since this massive granite was the coffin of Hapimen, it has been known to the Turks as the "Lover's Fountain," and used by them as a cistern. The Syenite sarcophagus of a standard-bearer, is marked 18. The chest of a royal sarcophagus that was taken from the mosque of St. Athanasius at Alexandria, and which contained the mummy of a king of the twenty-eighth dynasty, is marked number 10. On the exterior, the Sun is represented, attended by appropriate deities travelling through the hours of the day; and on the interior the visitor will recognise the quaint symbolic forms of the usual sepulchral gods and goddesses. The two remaining sarcophagi are those of a scribe and priest of the acropolis of Memphis, and a bard. That of the former, marked 3, is covered with the figures of Egyptian divinities and inscriptions to the deceased; that of the latter, in arragonite, is in the form of a mummy, like those first examined by the visitor. This coffin has five distinct lines of hieroglyphics engraved down the front, expressing a chapter of the funeral ritual: and the face bears evidence of having been gilt.

Having sufficiently examined these massive coffins, upon which the proudest undertaker of modern times must look humbly, and deplore the decline of his business as an art, the visitor should at once turn to other specimens of the sepulchral art of the ancient Egyptians. Of these, the most interesting are the sepulchral tablets, which are literally

ANCIENT EGYPTIAN TOMBSTONES.

Our modern tombstones record only the virtues of the dead. If future generations have to rely upon the revelations of our churchyards for facts connected with the people of modern times, they will write that we were all of us faultless as fathers, irreproachable as husbands, and devoted and self-sacrificial as children. Every tombstone is engraved with a catalogue of human virtues; and idlers wandering round about our country churches, find themselves surrounded by the ashes of fond husbands, innocent angels, and adored wives. These prattlings of sorrow have their happy significance, since they show the universal forgiveness that follows even the worst and basest of mankind to the grave. But viewed as historical records, tombstones are sadly erring guides. They tell histories of men, written by their mistresses or their children. The sculpture which adorns the graves of modern races in this country, generally represents urns, or weeping cherubims, broken flowers, or fractured columns, or grieving angels. These symbols of death and grief contrast often oddly with the hopeful scriptural sentences which they surmount. In some instances the occupation or calling of the deceased is typified on his tomb--the unstrung lyre telling the whereabouts of a dead musician; and a palette indicating the resting-place of a defunct painter. Little that is great in sculpture has of late marked burial-places.

The Egyptians, on the contrary, employed their choicest workmen to decorate their tombs. The visitor may, gathering together the scattered fragments from this saloon, picture to himself one of the massive solemn vaults of the old Egyptians--the walls decorated with sepulchral tablets, and beneath each tablet a massive sarcophagus, containing the mummy of the deceased whose actions the tablet records. Not altogether unlike the vaults of the present day, save that perishable materials suffice for modern notions; whereas the Egyptian provided comforts for the long, long rest, that, according to his creed, would elapse, before the mummy would shake off its bandages, and walk forth bodily once more. The Egyptian tablets, of which there are a great number scattered about the saloon, are, as the visitor will perceive, of small dimensions, but crowded with mystic hieroglyphics, and ornamental groups of the funereal deities and other subjects. The writing records the actions and the name of the deceased, together with various religious sentiments; and is therefore, in form and spirit, not unlike the modern epitaph. This resemblance is not so wonderful as it at first appears, seeing that the same circumstances acted upon the dictator of the old Egyptian epitaph, as those which make the modern widow eloquent. The most modern of the tablets in the present collection are those executed while Egypt was a Roman state, many are of the time of the Ptolemies, and one is believed to be of a date before the time of Abraham. This tablet is to the memory of a state officer: it is marked 212. The examination of the sarcophagi, will have led the visitor to the southern end of the saloon; and from this point he should once more turn to the north, and examine the sepulchral tablets on the eastern and western walls. He will notice that numbers of them exactly resemble one another in certain forms; that certain sepulchral scenes are frequently repeated, and that therefore the tablets cannot be said in many cases with certainty, to represent either passages in the life of the deceased, or symbolic images of his career.

First let the visitor remark, numbered 90, a basalt slab, presented to the museum by the Lords of the Admiralty. It is supposed to have been originally the cover of a stone coffin, in the time of the Ptolemies. It is remarkable for a Graeco-Egyptian recumbent figure, executed in bas-relief. The sepulchral tablets marked

128-9-31-32, are in calcareous stone. The first is that of a scribe, who is receiving a funeral offering from his son; the second is that of Akar-se, who is receiving the offerings of his bereaved family; the third, from Abydos, has similar representations of family offerings, and the fourth is that of the chief keeper of the cattle of Rameses II., named Hara, who prays to Horus, Isis, Nephthys, and Osiris. The first three tablets are dedicated to Isis. The visitor may also remark in this neighbourhood a fragment in bas-relief from the tomb near Gizeh, of Afa. Afa was a palace officer, who is supposed to have flourished about the period of the fourth dynasty. He is here represented, in company with various members of his family.

The next tablet to which the visitor should direct his attention is from Thebes, and is marked 139. It is that of a priest named Rames, who flourished during the reign of King Menephtah. Here the priest is represented in the act of adoring various deities, and accepting funeral honours from his family. The tablet marked 142 is of the time of the nineteenth dynasty. It bears an inscription referring to a governor of the Ramesseium, named Amen-mes. The next tablet that deserves particular remark is one in calcareous stone, from Abydos. It is in honour of a military chief of the twelfth dynasty, named Nechta. The pictorial embellishments represent the chief before a table of offerings, with his wife, mother, and nurse, seated before him. On the next tablet (144) a judge named Kaha, is adoring funeral deities, and receiving the usual honours from his family. Passing the tablet of the commander of the troops of the palace of Sethos I. (146) the visitor should pause before the interesting tablet marked 147. This tablet records the date of the birth and marriage of a female named Tai-em-hept, of the advent of her son Tmouth, and of her death which took place in the tenth year of the reign of Cleopatra. As the visitor progresses with his inspection of these tablets, he will be more and more struck with the minute revelations they afford of the subdivision of labour among the ancient Egyptians. For instance, one tablet (148) is that of a superintendent of the builders of the palaces of Thothmes IV. in Abydos; another (149) is that of a scribe of the royal quarries; a third (150) is that of a Theban judge, on the lower part of which are representations in yellow, in the style of the nineteenth dynasty, of the transport of the corpse, and other funeral ceremonies; a fourth (154) is that of a royal usher; a fifth is that of Pai, a queen's officer, among the illustrations of which a tame cynocephalus may be noticed. The tablet marked 159 is a very ancient specimen. It is that of Rutkar a priest, who is represented, in company with his wife, surveying the domestic occupations of his dependents. The tablet from Thebes, of Baknaa, a master of the horse in the reign of Sesostris is marked 164. Here the deceased is represented adoring a group of deities. The other tablets in this vicinity are chiefly of the time of Rameses II. or III, and are in honour of scribes and other functionaries immediately connected with the court. Two sepulchral tablets from Sakkara are interesting. That marked 184 is in honour of a priestess of Phtha named Tanefer-ho. The pictorial embellishments represent the priestess about to be introduced to Osiris and other deities by Anubis and other presiding spirits of the tomb. This specimen bears the date of the nineteenth year of the reign of Ptolemy Auletes. The second tablet from Sakkara (188) is that of an ancient pluralist named I-em-hept, who is represented introduced to Osiris and other deities by Anubis and his brother spirits or genii. The inscription below, in the vulgar character of the ancient Egyptians, is supposed to begin with the sixth year of Cleopatra. Near these tablets is one in dark granite, of a date before the twelfth dynasty (187) in honour of Mentu-hept, a superintendent of granaries and wardrobes. The next tablet to which the visitor's attention should be directed, is one crowded with symbolic animals and deities (191). It is that of a functionary named Kaha, who is adoring Chiun, standing on a lion, and grasping snakes, with Horus and other deities. Asi, a military chief and priest of a very remote period, is represented on the next tablet (192), with food before him, and the next (193) is that found before the great sphinx at Gizeh. On it the sun is represented, and a Greek inscription tells that it was erected in the time of Nero, by the inhabitants of Busiris to the Roman governor of Egypt, Tiberius Claudius Balbillus. The next tablet (194) is that discovered by Belzoni, near the temple of Karnak, on which a line of adoring deities are represented. The tablets marked 548, 9, 51 have no particular points of interest; the visitor may therefore at once pass to the group, most of which are coloured yellow, and are elaborately embellished, marked from 555 to 598. The first of these worth especial notice is that (555) of a Theban judge of the eighteenth dynasty. It is coloured yellow and the deceased is represented with the boat and the sun's disc above, and in company with his sister adoring the cow of Athor; the second (566) is in the form of a doorway, is of the nineteenth dynasty, is coloured, and is in honour of a conductor of the festival of Amen-ra; the third and fourth (557-8) are of earlier date, or the twelfth dynasty, and represent the deceased before tables of viands; the fifth tablet (560) is in honour of Her-chen, who is represented with his relations, and Phtah-kan, a scribe, also represented and similarly attended, all well finished and coloured; the three following tablets represent the deceased before tables of viands, coloured; the next (564) is that of the keeper of the treasury, or "silver abode," in the twelfth dynasty--he too is before a table of food in company with his relations; the next remarkable specimen is that marked 569, which is in honour of Athor-si, a functionary supposed to have been the superintendent of mines in the twelfth dynasty, who is here represented in one part before a table loaded with food, and in another part seated, with his hands humbly crossed upon his breast; the next tablets presenting particular points for remark are those of Eun-necht, (575) a superintendent of corn and clothing, of the twelfth dynasty. Senatef, chief of the palace to Amen-emha II., who is represented receiving a goose, a haunch, and other food from his relations. Eunentef, a chief and his son standing face to face, bearing wands and sceptres--a sculptor named User-ur, who is represented with his wives and parents, and upon which the square red lines used by the precise Egyptian artists are still visible on the unfinished parts. After several other tablets of the twelfth dynasty, is placed (584) a small square one of an earlier date in honour of Chen-bak, an architect, who is seated with his wife, receiving the duty of his children. Near this is a good specimen of old Egyptian bas-relief on calcareous stone, in honour of a palace officer named Amen-ha (586); and next to it (587) is a tablet in honour of a superintendent of all the gods, named Seraunut. Hereabouts also is the tablet from Thebes in honour of Hera, a royal scribe (588). On this tablet the deceased is represented bearing an appropriate feather sceptre before Nameses the ninth of the twentieth dynasty, who is seated on his throne, under the particular guardianship of the God of truth.

The tablet from Thebes marked 593 is that of a judge and his wife, and is dedicated to Osiris and Anup. Hereon, the lotus flower is represented, with corn and bread. The next tablet (594) is one in the shape of an altar of libations, and is dedicated to Amenophis I. and the queen Aahmes-Nefer-Ari. It is ornamented with representations of various foods, including vases of figs. In this neighbourhood are a few more tablets, including one on which are jars, water-fowl, and bread cakes, (596) and a fragment upon which the head of a king is traceable, marked 595. The visitor should also notice now the two early Saracenic tombstones presented by Dr.

Bowring. Having examined these, the more remarkable of the sepulchral tablets, or tombstones of the ancient Egyptians, the visitor, still lingering amid the funereal relics of long ages ago, should turn to the

EGYPTIAN SEPULCHRAL VASES.

As we explained when the visitor was in the Egyptian room, better known as the Mummy room, up stairs, in the course of his second visit, the ancient Egyptians, when they embalmed their dead, extracted the viscera, and deposited them, apart from the body, in four vases, over which the genii of the dead severally presided. Thus every mummy had, properly, four sepulchral vases; and the collection arranged in the saloon amply illustrates the varieties of ornament expended upon them. As the visitor has probably forgotten the particular parts assigned separately to the genii, it may be well to repeat here that Amset (who is human-headed,) had the stomach and large intestines under his especial protection Tuautmutf with his jackal-head presided over the heart and lungs; Kebhsnuf, with the fierce head of the widely worshipped hawk, took the gall, bladder, and liver, in charge; while the baboon-headed Hapi reserved to himself the care of the small intestines. There does not appear to have been any supernatural protector of the brains, which, as we have noticed, were drawn through the nose by the embalmer. These vases are of the most ancient times, chiefly before the advent of Alexander, after which event the people began to enclose the entrails of their dead in wax cloths, and fastening to the various parts the appropriate genius, to have been content to deposit them in the same case with the body. The vases which the visitor is about to examine are carved in different materials, the more costly and highly finished being of arragonite, and the less important, in wood, stone, or clay. They are all ornamented with appropriate inscriptions, consisting of exhortations of the deities to the dead, or comforting syllables from the genii of the intestines to the departed. The visitor will not care to examine all these vases in detail, nor would any purpose be served were the unscientific spectator to hover in this corner for a whole day; it is sufficient for him to understand the passage these vases occupy in the ancient history of Egypt, and to notice cursorily the degree of excellence displayed in the manufacture of them. He will find the hawk-head of Kebhsnuf in one direction, and the baboon-head of Hapi in another, and from these pictorial revelations he will know what part of a deceased Egyptian was deposited in each vase.

With these preliminary words we may leave him to examine the collection, reserving to ourselves the task of pointing his attention to one or two of the more remarkable specimens. First let the visitor notice the complete set of four, in arragonite, marked 614-17. These were for the internal parts of prince Amen-em-api, the eldest son of Rameses II., and as the visitor will notice, have severally their presiding genius, with sacred inscriptions. Another remarkable vase is that in arragonite marked 609, with its cover fashioned in the form of a human head, and the remains of an inscription which had been laid on with a thick kind of colour. That marked 629 with the jackal-head of Tuantmutf, bears an inscription in which the standard-bearer of Plato named Hara, part of whose body was inclosed, is reminded that the genius attends him. One (635) of arragonite has a green waxy paint, and belonged to a royal bow-bearer of the nineteenth dynasty, named Renfu. There is another complete set, which do not appear to have been opened, marked 636-39. The arragonite vases are the most expensive, and, as we have remarked the most highly finished; but the visitor may notice also those in coarser material.

Having sufficiently examined these vases, the visitor may take a general glance at the contents of the saloon, and prepare to examine the Sphinxes, and colossal figures that are crowded into it. In these he will recognise only colossal copies of many of the little figures he saw in the Mummy room up stairs. He will see huge granite representations of the strange gods and goddesses to which the ancients devoutly knelt; and in many of these forms he will trace a placid beauty that reveals often the soul of the sculptor fettered by the strange formulas of his religion. The visitor having examined the high reliefs on the tablets and sepulchral monuments of the ancient Egyptians, has now to examine the specimens that remain of their statuary. But first of

EGYPTIAN HUMAN STATUES.

In viewing cursorily the statuary of the ancient Egyptians, the investigator is first struck with the colossal proportions adopted by their sculptors. In those days, when iron was unknown, and when bronze was the manufactured metal, men contrived without the use of gunpowder, to remove vast masses of granite from their quarries, and to shape these masses into the form they chose. Had they a hero to whom they would pay honour? Forthwith his figure was immortalised in colossal granite. How these vast masses, when separated from the rock, and chiselled into statues, were removed to their destination in the court, or at the entrance of a temple, is a point not satisfactorily determined. That thousands of lives were spent, year after year, in the production of the vast monuments which now lie scattered in confusion about the valley of the Nile is certain; and some men contemplate this large expenditure of human muscle upon these rude masses, with a gentle melancholy that is not altogether called for. There was a spirit in the work that made it noble. And here it is well that the visitor shall see the opinion of a man whose conclusions were based upon profound erudition in his art, on the subject of ancient Egyptian art, artistically viewed. In his lectures on sculpture, Flaxman says, "Their (the Egyptian) statues are divided into seven heads and a half, the whole weight of the figure is divided into two equal parts at the *ospubis*, the rest of the proportions are natural and not disagreeable. The principal forms of the body and limbs, as the breasts, belly, shoulders, biceps of the arm, knees, shin-bones, and feet, are expressed with a fleshy roundness, although without anatomical knowledge of detail; and in the female figures these parts often possess considerable elegance and beauty. The forms of the female face have much the same outline and progression towards beauty in the features as we see in some of the early Greek statues, and, like them, without variety of character; for little difference can be traced in the faces of Isis, in her representations of Diana, Venus, or Terra, or indeed in Osiris, although sometimes understood to be Jupiter himself, excepting that in some instances he has a very small beard, in form resembling a peg. The hands and feet, like the rest of the figure, have general forms only, without particular detail; the fingers and toes are flat, of equal thickness, little separated, and without distinction of the knuckles; yet, altogether, their simplicity of idea, breadths of parts, and occasional beauty of form, strike the skilful beholder, and have been highly praised by the best judges, ancient and modern. In their basso-relievos and paintings, which require variety of action and situation, are demonstrated their want of anatomical, mechanical, and geometrical science, relating to the arts of painting and sculpture. The king, or hero, is three times larger than the other figures; whatever is the action, whether a siege, a battle, or taking a town by storm, there is not the smallest idea of perspective in the place, or magnitude of figures or buildings. Figures intended to be in violent action are equally destitute of joints, and other anatomical form, as they are of the balance and spring of motion, the force of a blow, or the just variety of line in the turning figure. In a word, their historical art was informing the beholder in the best manner they could, according to the rude characters they were able to make. From such a description it is easy to understand how much their attempts at historical representation were inferior to their single statues. What has been hitherto said of Egyptian sculpture, describes the ancient native sculpture of that people. After the Ptolemies, successors of Alexander the Great, were kings of Egypt, their sculpture was enlivened by Grecian animation, and refined by the standard of Grecian beauty in proportions, attitude, character, and dress. Osiris, Isis, and Orus, their three great divinities, put on the Macedonian costume; and new divinities appeared amongst them in Grecian forms, whose characteristics were compounded from materials of Egyptian, Eastern, and Grecian theology and philosophy."

First, to give the visitor an idea of the magnitude of the colossi of the ancient Egyptians, let him notice from the southern extremity of the saloon the gigantic cast of the face of Sesostris, placed against the southern wall of the central saloon. This face is a cast from a colossal statue of that great king of the Egyptians, which was one of four discovered by the energetic Belzoni, in front of the great temple of Ibsamboul in Nubia. It is a sitting figure, fifty feet high. These colossal figures of the great Egyptian monarch were plentiful throughout Egypt. As the visitor stands before this fragment of a stupendous piece of sculpture, he may recall to mind the points in the career of Giovanni Battista Belzoni. First, the boy helping his father to shave the beards of the Paduans; then the young adventurer flushed with hope, jogging on his way to Rome; then the grave young man, with his vast physical development shrouded in the monkish habit; then, in 1800, when Napoleon was busy in Italy, the monkish garments thrown aside, he wanders about the continent, stared at everywhere for his size and strength of limb; then as lecturer on hydraulic machinery, and exhibitor of feats of strength at Astley's Theatre; then, under the patronage of the Pasha, constructing a machine to water some gardens on the banks of the Nile; then engaged by the English Consul in Egypt, Mr. Salt, to prosecute some of the investigations into the monuments of antiquity, upon which that gentleman was expending much time and money; and here he is for the first time recognised in his true position. Of his labours as explorer of the tombs and temples of ancient Egypt few people are ignorant. How, dressed as a Turk, he transported the colossal granite bust of Memnon to Alexandria, and saw it safely on its way to England; how he penetrated into the Temple of Ibsamboul; how he patiently explored the rocks of the valley of Beban-el-Malouk, beyond Thebes to discover the entrances to tombs, and took exact copies of the thousands of figures he discovered upon sepulchral walls; how he penetrated into the bowels of the pyramid of Cephrenes, and found in the inmost chamber only the bones of a sacred bull; how he was honoured on his return to his native city; and how a desolate grave on an African shore was the end of his chapter--are matters of exciting adventure that are read by thousands of young people in the present day.

The visitor will see a strong family likeness in the colossal heads that are in the saloon. Proceeding northward from the southern end of the saloon, the visitor may rapidly notice the colossal fragments of the statues of kings and high officers, which are all distinctly marked. First, let the visitor examine two colossal heads (4-6), wearing the kingly head-covering, and said to resemble the features of Amenophis III., which were excavated under the superintendence of Mr. Salt, at Gournah; and then the visitor may turn to a fragment marked 9, which is a colossal fist, found among the ruins of Memphis by the French, and which fell, together with other valuable relics, into the possession of the English on the capitulation of Alexandria in 1801. This fist may well excite the admiration and respect of the most determined pugilist of the present day. Hereabouts also are a remarkable monument (12) found in the ruins of Karnak under the superintendence of Mr. Salt, placed upon a white stone pedestal in an angle of the wall of the great temple, and showing on each of its sides representations of Thothmes III. of the 18th dynasty, holding the hands of deities, said by some to be the moat curious specimen of Egyptian bas-relief in the Museum; a fractured colossus (14) in black granite, from Thebes, supposed to be part of a statue of Amenophis III.; the colossal head (15) discovered at Karnak by Belzoni in 1818, supposed to represent the features of Thothmes III.; the head and upper part of a statue of Sesostris, known as the Young Memnon. Before this, the most celebrated of the Egyptian specimens in the saloon, the visitor should pause to learn something of it, and notice its peculiarities for himself. Its name, 'Memnon,' is that given by the Greeks to many of the colossi which they saw scattered about the country when they made their way into Egypt. Memnon was the name given by the ancient Greek writers to an Egyptian hero who had a great reputation for his conquests, and was said to have done his share of work in the famous Trojan war. This name having been given indiscriminately to various statues, conveys no proof of their identity, since it represents only a mythical hero, whose fame reached Greece many centuries before our hero. Generally, this young Memnon is held to be a portrait of the great Sesostris, who was either the first or second Rameses; but some authorities declare that the weight of evidence goes in favour of Amenophis III., who was a pharaoh, or monarch, flourishing more than fourteen centuries before Christ. It is certain, however, that we have here a carefully-elaborated portrait of an Egyptian hero who flourished many centuries before our era. The features have all the prominent parts noticed by writers on Egyptian sculpture as characteristic of the Egyptian style. Here are the wonderfully high and prominent ears (which must have been invaluable peculiarities to Egyptian wits), the thick Ethiopian lips, the coarse nose, and the full eyes, all carefully and skilfully chiselled. Certainly, when we recall the time, realise fully the antiquity and the social state in which this great work was performed, we may see the sculptor's dawning soul in the majestic repose of this head. The lines are hard and stiff--have not the flow of the Parthenon decorations; but here is nothing mean or poor,--all large, solid, and carved with the force of a giant. The picturesque accounts of its transmission from the Memnonium at Thebes to Alexandria are familiar to the majority of readers, with the great Belzoni, with his marvellous strength and energy, urging on the workmen. "I cannot help observing," he tells us, "that it was no easy undertaking to put a piece of granite of such bulk and weight on board a boat that, if it received the weight on one side, would immediately upset; and, what is more, this was to be done without the smallest help of any mechanical contrivance, even a single tackle, and only with four poles and ropes, as the water was about eighteen feet below the bank where the head was to descend. The causeway I had made gradually sloped to the edge of the water, close to the boat, and with the four poles I formed a bridge from the bank into the centre of the boat, so that when the weight bore on the bridge it pressed only on the centre of the boat. The bridge rested partly on the causeway, partly on the side of the boat, and partly on the centre of it. On the opposite side of the boat I put some mats well filled with straw. I necessarily stationed a few Arabs in the boat, and some at each side, with a lever of palm-wood, as I had nothing else. At the middle of the bridge I put a sack filled with sand, that, if the Colossus should run too fast into the boat, it might be stopped. In the ground behind the Colossus I had a piece of a palm-tree planted, round which a rope was twisted, and then fastened to its ear, to let it descend gradually. I set a lever at work on each side; at the same time that the men in the boat were pulling, others were slackening the ropes, and others shifting the rollers as the Colossus advanced.

"Thus it descended gradually from the mainland to the causeway, when it sunk a good deal, as the causeway was made of fresh earth. This, however, I did not regret, as it was better that it should be so, than that it should run too fast towards the water; for I had to consider that if this piece of antiquity should fall into the Nile, my return to Europe would not be very welcome, particularly to the antiquaries; though I have reason to believe that some among the great body of its scientific men would rather have seen it sunk in the Nile than where it is now deposited. However, it went smoothly on board. The Arabs, who were unanimously of opinion that it would go to the bottom of the river, or crush the boat, were all attention, as if anxious to know the result, as well as to know how the operation was to be performed: and when the owner of the boat, who considered it as consigned to perdition, witnessed my success, and saw the huge piece of stone, as he called it, safely on board, he came and squeezed me heartily by the hand."

On the back of the statue are hieroglyphics describing the titles of Rameses. Marked 21, is a colossal black granite statue of the third Amenophis, also called Memnon, found also at Thebes in the year 1818. The next remarkable object to which the visitor's attention may be drawn is the sandstone statue of a monarch of the 19th dynasty, known as Leti Menephta II. (26), found at Karnak by Mrs. Belzoni. Here the characteristics of ancient Egyptian sculpture are strictly preserved, the figure having the arms close to the body, the hands resting upon the knees, and in the hands an altar, upon which is a ram's head. Hereabouts, also, is the lower part of a kneeling statue of Sesostris, supporting an altar, with the scarabaeus, or sacred beetle. Of the age of the 18th dynasty (of which Amenophis III. was the most notable monarch) is the restored group marked 29, which represents a guardian of the temple of Amenra and his wife, seated upon a throne ornamented with dedications to various deities. Having glanced at the limestone bust (30), from Gournah, of a statue to a king, the visitor may turn to a group (31) which represents an ecclesiastic, with his sister (who is a priestess), and his little son, a priest to Amenophis II.--the sister holding a bunch of lotus flowers. This group was found in a tomb near Thebes.

A headless statue, marked 35, with red colouring matter upon it, extracted from a sepulchre in the neighbourhood of the pyramids of Gizeh, is the next remarkable object deserving the general visitor's notice; and hereabouts, also, is another group, in the old Egyptian style (36), of an officer seated beside a female relation. Passing some remarkable objects which remain for notice under a separate head, and the lower part of a statue of Sesostris from Abydos (42), the visitor should next pause before a figure marked 43. This black granite statue is that of a queen of the 18th dynasty, and mother of the great Amenophis III. She is represented, as the visitor will perceive, seated upon a throne. A vulture, in an Athor-headed boat, hovers over her; and upon the boat the learned may read her name and dignities. Passing the upper part of a grey granite statue, representing a king, probably of the 12th dynasty (44), which was found in the neighbourhood of Gizeh, the visitor should halt before the statue of an Egyptian scribe, marked 46. This sitting figure is loaded with symbols. The pectoral plate suspended from his neck describes the dignities of the great Sesostris; in his right hand is a symbol of life, and in his left he holds a blade of corn. Near the scribe the visitor will notice a heavily-draped figure of black basalt, with the arms solemnly crossed, which was excavated from behind the Memnon at Thebes. This statue represents a military chief of the early part of the 18th dynasty, named Banofre. The figure numbered 51 is that of a prince named Anebta, who lived in the 18th dynasty: it is of calcareous stone, and was found at Thebes. The two next statues are those of a royal scribe of the 19th dynasty, and an officer connected with the libations to the god Amen-ra, both from Thebes. Two fragments, marked respectively 54 and 55, are the feet of a statue, and a colossal arm in red granite belonging to the colossal head, conjectured to be that of Thothmes III., found in the sand in the Karnak part of Thebes. Having examined these ponderous fragments, the visitor should next notice the colossal red granite statue of Sesostris found at Karnak (61), the kingly rank of the monarch being marked by the hat and the royal apron; and the upper part of a statue of the same monarch wearing the Pschent or crown of the Pharaohs, and holding a crook and whip. The small statue of Bet-mes, a state officer of the sixth dynasty, found in a tomb at Gizeh, is remarkable for its extraordinary antiquity; and in this neighbourhood, also, is a statue of an Ethiopian prince of the time of the great Rameses, named Pah-ur, which was found by Belzoni in Nubia. The figure is kneeling, and holding an altar. Passing the fragment, in grey granite, of a monarch of the 18th dynasty (75), the visitor may pause before another object taken from the French (81). It is the statue, from Karnak, of a high priest of Amen-ra, seated, holding an ear of corn, and, like his companions in stone, resting his arms upon his knees. Another fragment, of green basalt, may be passed (83), which is from a comparatively modern statue--that of a chamberlain in the reign of Apries, of the 26th dynasty; and then the visitor should pause before a white stone statue of the Ptolemaic period (92), which represents a priest of the god Chons, or Hercules, holding an altar upon which is a figure of the god; and hereabouts, also, he may remark another specimen of white stone sculpture, being the colossal bust of a queen of the 18th or 19th dynasty (93). Passing another fragment of a statue of the great Rameses, the visitor should next direct his attention to a dark granite statue, mutilated, of a high military officer, supposed to have flourished about the 12th dynasty. Among other fragments hereabouts, the visitor should not fail to examine the fragment (104) found in Alexandria, at the base of Pompey's Pillar, upon which are clearly traceable the figure of the great Rameses, being crowned by divinities, and a list of his dignities; the red granite colossal fist (106), presented to the Museum by Earl Spencer; and a curious fragment, which represents parts of a royal scribe, with his writing slab attached to his leg (103). Passing the curious double statue (110), of a State officer of the time of the eleventh Rameses, the visitor should once more halt before a basalt statue of a functionary (111), of the 26th dynasty, found in 1785, in the Natron Lakes, near Rosetta, and a granite group (113), representing, side by side, a chief, and a royal nurse, with the chief's daughter. Amid another group of fragments, the visitor should remark particularly an arragonite torso (121); the upper part of an officer, holding a standard (122); and a red granite bust of a monarch wearing the neumis (125). A small black basalt statue, of the period of the 26th dynasty (134) should be noticed. The figure, that of a palace officer, is kneeling, and has dedications to the deities. Further on is a statue of the third Thothmes, of the 18th dynasty (168), the head of which has been restored. Here the visitor should remark the nine bows which symbolise the enemies of the Egyptians. Having thus far noticed the collection of statuary which represent human beings, the visitor will gladly turn to those strange revelations of the ancient Egyptian mind developed in the

EGYPTIAN SPHINXES.

In these strange conglomerations of various races of animals--the lions with human heads and hawks' heads--there is generally preserved that majestic repose, and that mighty force of execution, which rescue the most incomprehensible of the ancient Egyptian monuments from contempt. Not at all farcical or barbarous could the effect have been, when the Egyptian approached his place of worship through an avenue formed by rows of these colossal sphinxes--all grandly fashioned and full of majesty. Mr. Long says: "Most speculations on the origin of the compound figure, called a sphinx, appear unsatisfactory; nor, indeed, is it an easy matter for the modern inhabitants of Western Europe to conceive what is meant by the symbolical forms which enter so largely into the ancient religious systems of the Eastern world. It seems to us altogether an assumption without proof, that either the andro-sphinx, or the sphinx with the female head, ought to be considered as the original type of this compound figure. The sphinx differs from other compound figures, which occur very often in the Egyptian pictorial representations, in always having the body of a lion, or, it may be, a panther, or some such animal as might be considered a symbol of strength and courage. The whole history of our species bears testimony to that tendency of the human mind, when not restrained and guided by better knowledge, to pourtray in some visible form its conceptions of Deity. However far many superior minds of the heathen world might advance, in deducing from the contemplation of all around them more correct views of the goodness and wisdom of an all-ruling power, these were ideas far too refined for the mass, who felt the want of something more apparent to the senses--something on which the mind could repose from vain imaginings and real fears. Hence the Deity was invested with various forms of familiar objects, under which he was venerated as a protector and friend, or feared as an avenging and angry power. Under the form of a ram, and the name of Ammon, we find a deity worshipped along the banks of the Nile, from the temple of the ancient Meroe to the sand-girt oasis of Siwah. The mild and benignant expression of the sacred ram would indicate the diffusion of tranquillity and peace, nor would the essential value of the symbol be changed by finding the head of the ram placed on human shoulders, or attached to the body of a lion. In the first case it would, in accordance with the Egyptian tradition of gods having assumed the forms of animals, commemorate, as in the Hindoo mythology, an incarnation of the superior power;

and in the second, the union of strength and courage with mildness and the arts of peace. The crio-sphinx, then, belongs to the Ammonian mythology, and is a distinct symbol from the andro-sphinx and female sphinx, which, probably, are connected with the worship of Osiris and Isis." Something of the effect may be comprehended from the two large red granite lions which mark the southern boundary of the saloon (1-34.) They are of the time of the third Amenophis, and were discovered at Mount Barkal by Lord Prudhoe, in 1829. As specimens of the mechanical skill of ancient Egyptian sculptors, they are worth particular remark. Here there is little of that angular stiffness characteristic of the statues the visitor has already examined. And now, making one more progress through the saloon, the visitor may rapidly notice the varieties of strange animal forms--all of which, in ancient Egypt, had their religious meaning. They were, at all events, symbols of divine instincts, and for this reason a deep interest rises in the modern mind in the contemplation of their proportions and expression. The figure numbered 7 is a colossal head of a ram, emblematic of Amen-ra; that numbered 8, is Hapi, the god of the Nile of the period of the 22nd dynasty, with allegorical waterfowl and plants hanging from the altar he is holding; two strange figures of gryphons, or hawk-headed sphinxes, found by Belzoni in the great temple of Ibsamboul (11-13), and emblematic or Munt-ra, will next engage the visitor's attention; and from these specimens the visitor should turn to a black granite fragment of the Egyptian Diana--Pasht, of the time of Amenophis; but as he will have an opportunity of observing more finished representations of this popular divinity, he may at once pause before a second statue of this goddess, also of the time of the third Amenophis (37), where Pasht is represented in black granite, upon a throne, with the head of a lion, and in her hand the emblem of life. Hereabouts, also, are two specimens of the strange cynocephalus, or dog-headed baboon (38-40), sacred to the Hercules and Mercury of the Egyptian Pantheon. The figures marked 41-45 are two more specimens of Pasht, who appears to have been the most popular subject for the Egyptian sculptor's chisel; these are erect figures, holding lotus sceptres, and are both from Karnak. The figures marked 49, 50, 52, 53, 57, are all representations of the popular Pasht; in 52 she wears the disk of the sun. And now the visitor may well pause before a fragment marked 58. This is a piece of the beard of the Great Sphinx. Peeping above the sands which surround the famous pyramids of Gizeh, is the upper part of a man-headed sphinx. This sphinx is said to measure no less than 62 feet in height, and 143 feet in length; this Colossus has been plucked by the beard, and the result lies before the visitor. Hereabouts, in passing, the visitor may glance at another object wrested from the hands of the French (59). It is a fragment of a column in porphyry, supporting a colossal areonite hawk, sacred to the sun. More statues of Pasht! (60, 62, 63, of the 22nd dynasty; 65, 68, 69). A column found in a house at Cairo, the capital of which is formed in the shape of a lotus flower (64), deserves notice; also (70), the basalt statue of a god, conjectured to be Amen-ra, holding a small figure of a monarch of the 28th dynasty. More statues of Pasht (71, 2, 3, 6, 7, 9; 80, 4, 5, 7, 8, 9); and then the visitor may pause before the colossal scarabaeus, emblematic of the world and creation (74); and a broken sphinx, of Roman work (82). Not far off are deposited the legs of Truth (91), the goddess Ma of the Egyptians; some altars from Aboukir and Sais, that marked 135, from the Temple of Berenice, having steps leading to it; entrances to tombs (157), ornamented with figures; and more statues of Pasht, amongst them a colossal bust from a statue (521).

Having noticed these specimens, the visitor should pass into the lobby at the northern end of the saloon, to notice the two small obelisks placed here, brought from Cairo; they stood before a temple to Thoth. The hieroglyphics upon them are carefully executed, but these specimens give the spectator no idea of the colossal obelisks of ancient Egypt, of which that of Alexandria, 63 feet high, is a fair specimen. These obelisks were generally in pairs, and were placed on each side of the great entrance to Egyptian temples. Having returned to the saloon, the visitor should, before finally passing from it, notice the famous tablet of Abydos (117), found by Mr. Banks, in 1818, in the Temple of Abydos. It is the work of the great Sesostris, and the inscription on it is a record of his predecessors in the kingly office: hence it has been long an attractive object to chronologists. Also, before glancing at the few paintings, and closing the examination of this interesting saloon, the visitor should inspect the Rosetta stone (24), inscribed in three characters (of which one is Greek), by order of the high priests, recording the services of the fifth Ptolemy. And now, with a glance at the

EGYPTIAN FRESCOES,

the visitor should rapidly close his survey of this chamber. These are rude performances enough, and, as the visitor will see, bear a close resemblance to those we introduced to him in the Egyptian rooms up stairs. Mr. Long, while on the subject of Egyptian art, thus mentions their paintings:--"Sculpture and painting were closely allied, both among the Egyptians and in the old schools of Greece; and both arts were intimately associated with architecture. Sculptured and coloured figures formed in ancient Egyptian edifices the decoration and the finish of the larger masses of the architecture which served as a framework within which they were placed. The edifices, from their massy forms and the magnitude of their component parts, were well calculated to produce a general impression of grandeur; and this was not destroyed by the smaller decorated parts, which were always strictly subordinate to the general design, and were not, like it, comprehended at a glance, but required to be studied in detail.

"Painting, in the proper sense of the term, that of the representations of objects by colours on the flat surface, appears to be an art of less antiquity than that of sculpture. The Egyptians probably first coloured their reliefs and statues before they attempted to represent objects with colours on a flat ground. But, however this may be, paint was most extensively used by them, not only in making pictures, properly so called, but in painting the surfaces of tablets and temples, as well as colossal statues and sculptured figures of all kinds and sizes. Indeed, an Egyptian temple, in its complete state, bedizened with so many bright unmixed colours, must have been rather a curious object, and would hardly, perhaps, have pleased the taste of modern times; though, it must be admitted, that the effect of these colours under a brilliant sun would be very different from their appearance in such a climate as this. The pureness, permanence, and brilliancy of Egyptian colouring are the only qualities that we can admire; for they never, apparently, compounded colours so as to produce a greater variety from the simple colours. It has also been frequently remarked that they did not soften them off so as to form various degrees of intensity, or to make any attempt at contrasts of light and shade. This is probably true as to the representation of human figures, which are coloured pretty much in the same style that a child paints uncoloured engravings, making one part all red, another all blue, and so on, without any softening of the colours at their common boundary.

But in the representation of animals, as we shall afterwards observe, more care was taken in softening and blenching the colours, so as to produce a better representation of nature.

"The colours used in the painted relief, and on the stuccoes are black, blue, red, green, and yellow; these are always kept distinct and never blended. Of blue, they used both a darker and a lighter shade. Red was used to represent the human flesh, apparently from its being nearer the natural tint than any other simple colour; but many of their colours were evidently applied with a conventional meaning, for the representation of different races. The conquered people represented in the great temple of Abonsambel, or Ipsambul, have yellow bodies and black beards. In the grottoes of El Cab, the men are red, and the women yellow. Black men also sometimes appear in the paintings. The five colours above enumerated seldom occur all in one piece or picture; but in this matter there is perhaps no general rule. The Nubian temples have often a very rich colouring, as in the case of one at Kalapsche, where yellow, green, red, and blue, have all been used in painting the reliefs in one of the inner chambers; and in some single figures in this temple we may observe all these four colours.

"The materials of which the colours were made would no doubt change with the improvements in the arts; and after the Macedonian occupation of the country, new colours, both vegetable and mineral, may have been introduced. But the tombs of the kings at Thebes may undoubtedly be considered as containing specimens of ancient Egyptian colouring, as well as the painted reliefs in the oldest temples, and the colourings about the ancient mummies. By a careful examination of these specimens, we may attain a very adequate knowledge of the materials used, and of the mode of applying them." The first of these frescoes (169-170-1) are from the walls of a tomb of the western Hills of Thebes. The tomb is that of a scribe of the royal granaries and wardrobe, and the pictures represent the inspection of oxen by scribes, a scribe standing in a boat, the registration of the delivering of ducks and geese and their eggs. The fragment marked 175 represents an entertainment, with female instrumental performers; here (176) an old man is leaning upon a staff near a cornfield; there (177) is the square fish-pond woefully deficient in prospective; there is a second entertainment (179), where the wine is freely circulating; dancing is going on to music--the picture of a social evening enjoyed thousands of years ago;

and here, at a third entertainment (181), servants are bringing in wine and necklaces--a kind of hospitality to which, as regards the latter object, modern ladies would in no way object. The ancient Egyptian ladies had their bouquets, their ornaments, and their couches, and exacted a plainness of costume from their servants, as in the present time. On passing south from the Egyptian Saloon, between the two great lions, the visitor at once gains the central saloon, but without pausing here, or turning to the right into the tempting Phigalian and Elgin Saloons, he should proceed rapidly on his way to the south-western extremity of the building, at which point he will find himself at the entrance to the

LYCIAN ROOM.

In a few preliminary words we may indicate the points of Lycian history. Situated in Asia Minor, Lycia is said to have taken its name from the Athenian prince Lycus, who conquered it, and laid it open to his countrymen. This Greek period of its history was interrupted by Cyrus, who added it to the Persian empire about five centuries and a half before our era; it was only regained about two centuries after by Alexander the Great. It subsequently became a Roman province, then yielded to the Byzantine empire, and now owns the rule of the Turk. This eventful history gives an interest to the country that has excited the curiosity of the learned for ages. The period of its greatest prosperity ensued upon its being reconquered by Alexander, when it included no less than seventy cities, of which Xanthus was the capital. Of all these cities, only scattered ruins under Turkish villages now remain. Of Lycian remains it may be said nothing was known before Sir Charles Fellows started on his exploring expedition in 1838. One or two travellers had made some scattered observations with regard to the sites of ancient Lycian towns before that time, and their hints first drew the attention of the learned in this direction; but, we repeat, it cannot be said that anything was known of Lycian remains before Sir Charles pressed the soil of Asia Minor, and looked about for the sites of some of the seventy towns mentioned in ancient history. He succeeding in fixing the sites of many of the cities, including Xanthus, and on his return to England prevailed upon the government to send out vessels to bring home the remains he saw scattered about the rocky site of the ancient Lycian metropolis. Messrs. Spratt and Forbes subsequently added eighteen sites of towns to the list made by Sir Charles. The collection of sculpture now popularly known as the Xanthian marbles, are a few ruins gleaned from the rocky eminence which is the site of ancient Xanthus. These fragmentary remains of an ancient people consist chiefly of sculptures from their temples and their tombs; upon which, like the Egyptians, they appear to have expended a vast amount of labour, and to have employed their greatest artists. The Greek mind is clearly traceable in these Xanthian marbles,--the Greek imbued with local traditions and feelings. The first object that will attract the visitor's attention on entering the room, is the most remarkable of

LYCIAN TOMBS,

called the Harpy Tomb. This tomb, which occupied the highest point of the hill on which Xanthus stood, is described by Sir Charles Fellows in his account of the Xanthian marbles, published in 1843. The tomb was a square shaft, in one solid block, weighing no less than eighty tons. "Its height," says Sir Charles, "was seventeen feet, placed upon a base, rising on one side six feet from the ground, on the other but little above the present level of the earth. Around the sides of the top of the shaft were ranged bas-reliefs in white marble, about three feet three inches high; upon these rested a capstone, apparently a series of stones, one projecting over the other; but these are cut in one block, probably fifteen or twenty tons in weight. Within the top of the shaft was hollowed out a chamber, which, with the bas-relief sides, was seven feet six inches high, and seven feet square. This singular chamber had probably been, in the early ages of Christianity, the cell of an anchorite, perhaps a disciple of Simeon Stylites, whose name was derived from his habitation, which, I believe, we have generally translated as meaning a column, but which was more probably a *stele* like this. The traces of the religious paintings and monograms of this holy man still remain upon the backs of the marble of the bas-reliefs." By reference to the model of the tomb, of which the bas-reliefs are in the room (1), the visitor may verify the remarks of Sir Charles, who goes on to say that the monument was never finished, having been only half polished, and that it bears the traces of a shake from an earthquake. The general conjecture is that the tomb is the labour of a Lycian Greek sculptor. The subjects of the bas-reliefs have been variously interpreted: they decorated, as the visitor will perceive by reference to the model, the four sides of a square shaft. First, let the visitor turn to the western face, marked (B). Here the scene represented is supposed to be Juno holding a cup before the sacred cow Io, and Epaphus, Aphrodite, and the three Charites, which have been interpreted also as the three Seasons, and the Erinnyes or Furies. The eastern side marked (A), is supposed to represent Tantalus, bringing the golden dog stolen from Crete to Pandarus in Lycia: Neptune seated, with a man leaning on a crutch, and a boy offering a bird before him, and Amymone and Amphitrite behind him; and AEsculapius seated with Telesphorus in front, and two of the Graces behind him. The northern side (C), shows at the corners, two Harpies making off with two of the daughters of Pandarus, while their sister Aedon, on her knees, is deploring their abduction. Here, too, is a god seated, conjectured to be Pluto, holding a helmet with the help of another figure, and having a wild animal under his chair. The south side (D), discloses two Harpies bearing off the daughters of Pandarus; and in the centre is a god, to whom a female figure is offering a dove. By the side of these bas-reliefs, the visitor cannot fail to remark the tomb of a Satrap of Lycia from Xanthus. From the fact of horses being clearly traceable among the figures sculptured upon this interesting relic, Sir Charles Fellows christened it the Horse Tomb, and by this appellation it is popularly known. Its strange shape, with its highly decorated roof and plain base, makes it an object of curiosity to most visitors. It appears to be of the time of the Persian dominion in Lycia, and was, as two inscriptions record, erected by the satrap Paiafa. Upon the roof are groups of fighting warriors, and at each side are figures in chariots and four. Sphinxes occur in the lower sculptures, and on the north side below, is a mixed combat of foot and horse soldiers; and the Satrap Paiafa himself, attended by four figures, is here represented. The roof is drained by water-spouts in the shape of lion's heads. The visitor, having now examined the two most remarkable remains of Lycian tombs in the room, should rapidly notice the fragments of sepulchres placed here and there, but legibly numbered. First, let him remark (17-21), a frieze conjectured to be from a tomb found inserted in the wall of the Acropolis of Xanthus. Here he will find in bas-relief a procession consisting of a horse and horseman, priest and priestesses with wands, an armed female figure, and two chariots, with youthful charioteers and old men. A triangular fragment of a tomb will next occupy his attention (23); this has distinct vestiges of colour, and represents a male and female figure separated by an Ionic column, surmounted by an harpy, and other fragments in the immediate neighbourhood; (24-27) have representations of the Sphinx, with a woman's head, wings, and the body of a lion, as the daughter of the Chimaera, from the Xanthian Acropolis. A curious relic is the *Soros*, discovered placed on the top of one of the Xanthian pillar tombs. Here, amongst the bas-reliefs, the visitor will notice a man stabbing an erect lion; a lion playing with its young; and a figure on horseback followed by a pedestrian; and on the next fragment (32), a lioness is again represented fondling her progeny. The roof of a tomb (143), closely resembling that which covers the Horse Tomb, is worth observing. It is part of the tomb of an individual named Merewe, from Xanthus, and the scenes represented include that of an entertainment, divinities, and sphinxes, warlike encounters, and on the sides Bellerophon attacking the Chimaera. Those casts marked (145-149), may next engage the visitor's attention. They were taken from a tomb carved in solid rock at Pinara, and include the frieze, upon which warriors are carved leading captives, the walls representing a walled city, and the Gorgons' heads which decorated the extremities of the dentals. The three next casts that demand particular remark (150-152), were taken from the decorations of a rock tomb at Cadyanda. To the learned these groups are particularly interesting, because the figures are accompanied with inscriptions in the Greek, as well as the pure Lycian language. The first cast is that from the panel of the tomb door, upon which Talas is represented standing: the second represents a group of females; and the third an ancient entertainment with figures reclining on couches with children; a figure playing the double flute, and to the right a nude figure called Hecatomnas. Six casts from tombs hereabouts (153-6), exhibit inscriptions, two of which are in two languages--the Lycian and the Greek, declaring that the owners have built the tombs for themselves and their relations; the second marked 156, in the Lycian language, expresses a threat that a fine will be imposed on any person who may violate the tomb. Bellerophon, riding on Pegasus, may be remarked launching his dart at the Chimaera, upon the cast (158); nymphs are dancing upon the gable end marked (160); and upon that marked (161), which is a cast from the gable end of a tomb discovered at Xanthus, near the Chimaera tomb, two lions are represented devouring a bull. The casts of the sculptures which decorate an ancient rock tomb at Myra, are interesting. Here a young man, attended by a boy, is offering a flower to a veiled woman, attended by two women; in another part a boy attends with wine upon a figure, conjectured to be that of Pluto, and a veiled female form, supposed to be either Proserpine or Venus, is draped by an attendant, in the vicinity of a nude youth. The remains of sarcophagi are marked (168-171). The first of these are the relics of a Roman sarcophagus, discovered in a mausoleum, containing three other sarcophagi, at Xanthus. On the top have been reclining figures of a male and female, and at the sides combats of warriors. The next relic is a fragment of a sarcophagus, amongst the ornaments of which boys are shown at play; and the third fragment discovers the lower part of the representation of a hunt. An exceedingly explicit inscription is that marked (176,) and found at Uslann, near the mouth of the Xanthus, which informs modern generations that some two thousand years ago, Aurelius Jason, son of Alaimis, and Chrysion, daughter of Eleutherus, purchased a tomb for themselves, in the thirteenth month Artemisios, during the priesthood of Callistratus, and dwelling upon this piece of information, which is striking as a voice from the tomb of unknown people speaking to us of the present century, not from any remarkable deed achieved by Aurelius Jason, but simply because his name occurs upon his tomb, plainly written in his own language. A strange immortality! Having examined these relics of the ancient tombs of Lycia, the visitor should take a general glance at

LYCIAN SCULPTURE.

The time during which the Lycians may be said to have enjoyed their highest civilisation dates from about five centuries before our era, up to the period of the Byzantine empire. During this long interval, most of the monuments of which this room contains some remarkable specimens were conceived and executed. Of the sculpture, not immediately illustrative of tombs, in the Lycian room, the most interesting, undoubtedly, is that gleaned from the site of an ancient building on the Acropolis of ancient Xanthus, by Sir Charles Fellows. Passing a few fragments, including that marked (33), from Xanthus, which represents the foreparts of two lions issuing from a square block, the visitor should pass at once to the model of a Xanthian Ionic peristyle building, surrounded by fourteen columns and ornamented with statues, made under the direction of Sir Charles Fellows, from the remains found on the site of the original building, which lie about the room, and which the visitor is about to examine. The original building was thirty-five feet in height, measuring from the pediment to the base. Its object has been variously stated, but cannot be said to be clearly and satisfactorily known. Of the conjectures which have obtained certain credit, we may mention that which described it as a trophy raised, in 476 B.C., to celebrate the subjugation of Lycia by the Persians; and that which describes the subject of the decorative sculptures as that of the suppression of the revolt of the Cilicians by the Persian Satrap of Lycia. The remains of this mysterious building are ranged in groups about the room; and the visitor will observe indications of the flow of the lines, and the artistic grace, which subsequently marked Grecian sculpture from every other on the face of the earth. Here it is not impossible to recognise the Greek mind: far below that of the decoration of the Parthenon, it is true; but yet elegant and thoughtful. The groups of sculpture marked (34-49) are the sculptures of the broader frieze which, it is conjectured, surrounded the base of the building. Here are represented a series of warlike encounters in which the Greek arms are prominent--their helmets, crests, and Argolic bucklers; while other soldiers are represented nearly nude, and in some instances wearing the Asiatic pointed cap. This frieze undoubtedly represents the Greeks at war with Asiatic tribes. The fragments of the narrow frieze which bordered the upper part of the frieze are marked from 50 to 68. The first four fragments represent the attack of a town, supposed to be the Lycian town Xanthus. Here the besiegers may be observed scaling the wall, and the officers cheering on the men. The five following fragments represent various scenes of warfare between Greeks and Asiatics. Then a walled city is represented, with the heads of a besieged party looking over the ramparts; then a figure of a Satrap occurs (62), supposed to be that of the Persian conqueror of Lycia, Harpagus, who is screened with an umbrella held by a slave, which is the emblem of his sovereignty, and is in the act of receiving a deputation from the besieged city. The next two fragments represent a sally from the besieged town; and upon the 67th fragment is some carving supposed to illustrate the retreat of the besieged to their city. The groups marked (69,70,74) are fragments of the capping-stones of the east front of the base, and columns and fragments of columns from the peristyle. Those groups, however, marked (75-84), which consist of the statues originally placed in the intercolumniations of the building, are figures of divinities, with various symbols at their feet, as the dolphin, the halcyon, &c., and are meant to represent, by the flow of the drapery, that they are flying through the air. They have been variously interpreted, but never satisfactorily; some authorities asserting that they were meant to celebrate the arrival of Latona at Xanthus, and others that they symbolise the great naval victory over Evagoras. Passing over one or two unimportant groups of fragments, the visitor should next examine the remains of the narrow frieze (95-109), upon which an entertainment is represented--the guests, perfectly used to luxuries, reclining upon couches, and taking wine to the strains of female musicians; also, a sacrifice of various animals. Passing the coffers of the ceiling (106-109), the visitor should next examine the remains of another narrow frieze, where a Satrap is represented receiving presents; and bear and boar hunting scenes occur. The fragment marked (125) is the eastern pediment, sculptured in relief with various figures; and that marked (126) is half of the western pediment sculptured with figures of six foot-soldiers. The groups numbered (132-135) are fine specimens of Lycian sculpture: on the first a draped female figure is shown in rapid flight; and on the second, youths are shown bearing off women. The group marked (138) is one of the samples of the roof-tiles with which the building was covered in. Two crouching lions (139, 140), supposed to have occupied intercolumnar space in the building, are the last of the fragments. These fragments, however, together with Sir Charles's interesting model, and the landscape (also in the room), realise more vividly to the mind of the general spectator the ancient Xanthus, than all the other detached and solitary fragments. Near the two lions just mentioned are the paws of another lion, and a fragment, found near the Harpy Tomb, of a crouching warrior and bull. Having noticed these, the visitor may occupy himself for a few minutes with the fragments of Byzantine architecture (177-183). These remains were discovered amidst the ruins of a Christian village; and, it is conjectured, were buried by an earthquake. These objects being discussed, the visitor should repair to the glass case at the end of the room, and examine some small curiosities from the Xanthian Acropolis, which are placed therein. These consist chiefly of a Parian-marble torso of a Venus; the left elbow of a female, and the left side of a female head, in Parian marble, found built into the walls of the Acropolis; leaden and iron cramps found in the oldest sculptures of the Acropolis; four small lamps; vases; a cup; fragments of glass vessels; fragment of a vase of the Byzantine period, stamped with a cross; bronze vessels; lead grating for a drain pipe; a fragment of a terra cotta amphora, inscribed, in the Doric dialect, with the name of Hippocrates; fragments of painted cement from early Christian buildings--all found in the excavations made for the ruins of the building of which the model and fragments have lately been noticed. Some sickles, a leaden weight, fragments of glass windows, and terra cotta fragments, also included in the glass-case, were discovered among the ruins of the houses, buried by the fall of the great building. And in this case, also, are some curiosities from Pinara, including fragments of human bones, tiles, and cement, all amalgamated by a deposit of lime filtering through the rock of a tomb; cement used to line a water cistern, and to block up the door of a rock-tomb. With an examination of these relics, the visitor will close his inspection of the Lycian remains, and proceed at once to the

ASSYRIAN REMAINS.

Having examined the monumental remains of the Egyptians and the ancient inhabitants of Persia, the visitor, in order to complete a general impression of the sculptures of remote antiquity, should now direct his attention to the remains recently discovered on the site of ancient Nineveh and Nimroud. Most readers have read something of the history of Assyria, of the effeminate Sardanapalus, of Semiramis, and of the more fabulous Ninus. These three names are the three landmarks of Assyrian history; and the long lapses of time which separate them are shrouded in mystery, and up to late years have been filled up only by fanciful histories but slenderly based on fact. Men have written confidently on the fall of the Assyrian empire, and of its invasion by the Medes; but the discrepancies of rival authorities, who differ as much as ten centuries in their dates according to Mr. Layard, show how insufficient were the materials upon which they pretended to found histories. Where was the site of Babylon? where that of the renowned Nineveh? These questions were often mooted by antiquaries. Mounds of earth were long observed by travellers in Assyria and Babylonia; and one of these, which was formed by a mass of ruined brickwork, was heralded to the world as the remains of the tower of Babel! But the ruins of the great Assyrian capital were for a long time unobserved. For many years had travellers to modern Mosul looked with wondering eyes at gigantic mounds of earth that lay opposite the city. The first traveller who did more than take a cursory view of these mysterious hillocks was Mr. Rich, who, on his way from Kurdistan to Baghdad in 1820, crossed the river, and arrived at the mounds; visited what the inhabitants asserted to be Jonah's tomb on the summit of one of them; saw inscribed relics in the houses of the adjacent village. Among the fragments on the largest mound he picked up some bricks with cuneiform[8] characters upon them, and fragments of pottery; and on a subsequent occasion he found a small stone chair. He left these mounds without suspecting that he had been treading above the palaces of the ancient Assyrian monarchs--that he had been over ancient Nineveh. But the ground was too fruitful in remote traditions to remain altogether unexplored in this century. The lands watered by the Tigris and the Euphrates, where the early Asiatic colonies of Scripture were founded, and where Nimrod, the grandson of Ham, flourished and founded Babel, and whence, according to Scripture, Asshur went forth to build Nineveh, are interesting ground. Of these great Assyrian towns it was natural to seek some ruins. Of all these cities, however, founded so far back before authentic history begins, only Nineveh, which flourished many centuries later, and of which we have always had more authentic histories than those of any other Assyrian city, attained to a comparatively modern prosperity and renown. The records of this magnificent city, from which historians have derived their information, describe its walls as reaching no less than two hundred feet in height, and broad enough to be a chariot-way. These walls were sixty miles in circumference, and guarded by fifteen hundred towers; and in the eighth century before the Christian era the city is estimated to have included a population of more than half a million souls. But many centuries before this, Nineveh was a wonderful city, of which the great monarch Ninus was king, and of which his celebrated wife, Semiramis, was afterwards queen. Ninus is the reputed founder of the Assyrian empire, and to him the magnificence of the capital is chiefly attributed. He is the Sesostris of Assyrian history, and is supposed to have flourished about twelve centuries before our era. The names of many Assyrian monarchs occur in the Sacred Writings: Sennacherib, who, seven centuries before our era, besieged Jerusalem and invaded Judea; and Shalmanasaar, who carried away the ten tribes of Israel. Later, the sovereignty of the Assyrian nation was transferred to Babylon by Nebuchadonosor; and afterwards the Medes and Babylonians laid the magnificent Nineveh in ruins, over which, many centuries afterwards, Herodotus wandered wonderingly, and endeavoured to glean from the pitiful wreck an idea of the bygone glory. The centre of the ancient Assyrian empire was the present Turkish province of Mosul; and hereabouts the researches of travellers have therefore been concentrated. Opposite Mosul, the capital of the province, are the two mounds which Mr. Rich hastily explored in 1820. These mounds have long formed the subject of animated controversies; but it was not before the year 1842 that any serious attempt was made to penetrate beneath the grass that covered them. In this year M. Botta, the French consul at Mosul, made some insignificant opening, but without discovering any remarkable remains; and rumours having reached him from Khorsabad, a few miles off, of some remains there, he caused some vigorous excavations to be made there, and, aided by his government, contrived to lodge an excellent collection of Assyrian sculptures in the Louvre. About this time Mr. Layard was travelling through the Turkish Asiatic provinces; and in the course of his wanderings paid considerable attention to the mounds situated at Nimroud and near Mosul. Convinced that under these hillocks lay precious relics of antiquity, he procured an official letter to the Pasha of Mosul, and in 1845 repaired to Nimroud, and hired Arabs to make excavations in the mounds there. Even the first day's search disclosed valuable slabs ornamented with bas-reliefs and inscriptions in the cuneiform character, of the remotest antiquity, dating so far back as nineteen centuries before our era, and conjectured to be part of the ruins of the chief palace of Nimroud, destroyed about twelve centuries before our era. If so, this point was the original centre of the great city of Nineveh--that part said to have been built by Asshur; while the surrounding mounds of Mosul, Khorsabad, and Kouyunjik, cover ruins of a later date. Of Mr. Layard's discoveries in Assyria, that room, which the visitor should now enter (called the NIMROUD ROOM), is full. The room, as the visitor will at once perceive, is divided into eleven compartments--the first being that to the left on entering. Here he will begin his inspection of

ANCIENT ASSYRIAN SCULPTURE.

The first slabs to which the visitor will direct his attention in the compartment (1), are from the north-west edifice, excavated from the Nimroud Mound, which Mr. Layard conjectures to be the most ancient of all the Assyrian ruins, dating, as we have stated, so far back as nineteen centuries before our era. On one slab the visitor will notice two standing draped figures, divided by the sacred tree, or tree of life, generally worshipped in the East, and adhered to in the religious systems of the Persians, here more like trellice-work than a tree, holding chaplets in their hands; on two other slabs figures with the sacred tree; and on a fourth we recognise the symbol of royalty among the ancient nations of Asia Minor, the umbrella borne by an eunuch over a monarch, who is represented returning from the chase, to the airs played by two musicians. Five figures are respectfully meeting him, and a dead animal lies at his feet. These specimens of the state of art in Asia, twenty-seven centuries ago, may well excite the curiosity of all classes of spectators. Proceeding to the second compartment, the visitor will find eight more slabs, the first of which from the north-west edifice, represents a battle-piece. Here warriors are discharging their arrows, the king with the winged symbol of divinity in a circle above him is proceeding at full gallop, and a dead figure lies near him pierced with arrows. This scene is continued on the second slab, where there are two chariots, each containing two figures, and one decorated with the ferouher, or divine symbol. A siege is represented upon the third slab. Here the besiegers are applying the battering ram; figures are falling from the walls, while from the three tiers of battlements the besieged are vigorously discharging arrows. The visitor will notice the figures of two bow-men on the fourth slab, before a lake, with part of a tower in the distance, and the next three slabs have representations of the fall of the city, picturesquely indicated. The deserted battering rams stand near the walls; female prisoners are leaving the town, drawn by three oxen; eunuchs are driving away the cattle of the vanquished, and conducting prisoners with their hands bound.

The third compartment is occupied with slabs, the sculptured subjects of which closely resemble those just described, except that marked 7, where the king, in his chariot, is hunting the lion. He has had some success, as one royal beast lies dead under his horse's feet, and another is pierced by four arrows.

The fourth compartment contains some interesting slabs. The first two represent one continuous subject. First, the visitor will notice the figure of an Assyrian monarch, with his chariots and attendants behind him, holding up arrows in token of peace to an advancing group, the first figure of which is addressing the king, while on one side a eunuch is introducing four captives. The two following slabs present illustrations of the crossing of a river. A boat, in which the royal chariot containing the king is deposited, is being dragged by two men ahead, while others are rowing, and behind follow horses and smaller boats. In their delineations of battles, the Assyrians were sagacious, since they vividly pourtrayed the horrors of war, by carving dead figures in the back ground, with birds preying upon them, even before the fray is over. Of this kind of vivid representation the visitor has a specimen on the next slab; where, while warriors are discharging their arrows, a dead soldier is being devoured by a bird in the back-ground, while another, as a pleasant suggestion of the impending fate of the survivors, hovers above their heads. The passage of troops over mountainous country, or through jungle, is the subject illustrated in the two following slabs (6,7); these are from Khorsabad, and include an inscription with the name of the monarch of that locality. Two slingers appear on the eighth slab, with archers attacking. On the next slab (9) enemies are represented in full flight, with a chariot containing two figures in hot pursuit: and on the last slab in this compartment, a city, with four battlemented towers is represented, with women standing between the towers, and chariots outside the walls.

Some curious fragments of large figures are included in the fifth compartment. First, there is a bearded head covered with a horned cap; also, the bust of a figure with the conical cap of the Assyrians: then the head of a figure, with traces of paint yet upon it, crowned with a tiara of rosettes. Here also is a fragment representing a king attended by a strange symbolical winged figure holding the popular fir-cone in his right hand, and in his left a basket, of which the visitor will remark a perfect specimen presently. The examination of these fragments will conduct the visitor to the end of the room, and before turning to examine the contents of the opposite compartments, he should pause to notice an obelisk placed hereabouts, which was dug from the centre of the great mound at Nimroud. It is seven feet in height, and is inscribed elaborately in the cuneiform character. On its surface are also engraved representations of various animals bearing presents.

The visitor will now turn and proceed back towards the door, examining, by the way, the compartments on his left hand. The firs
t of these, or the sixth compartment, contains, in addition to the fragments of figures including the head and shoulders of a king, and the upper part of an eunuch, two slabs (1,2) upon which is represented that fruitful subject of the Assyrian sculptor's chisel, the siege of a castle. The castle, which is represented in the middle of the battle-piece, and at the water's edge, is attacked by soldiers on all sides. The vigour of the assailants is well described. On the left the king directs the attack, with weeping women behind him; the walls are being scaled by ladders; the besieged are hurling stones from the ramparts, and casting fire upon a tower and ram, while the assailants are quenching the flames with water, and two figures are quietly picking holes in the walls in another direction. Hereabouts the visitor should notice, placed against the window, a pastoral subject--a man driving cattle. Upon the next slab, a war chariot in full speed, passing over a dead lion, is represented; and on the sixth and last slab of the compartment is another battlepiece. Here the besieged castle is

How to See the British Museum in Four Visits

surrounded by water; one of the besieged is holding arrows aloft in token of peace, while figures, on inflated skins, swim towards the walls, and soldiers from the banks are aiming arrows at them.

The fragments in the seventh compartment may be easily understood from the descriptions of previous slabs. The eighth compartment contains some remains which demand particular notice. The first slab introduces us to a knowledge of the interiors of Assyrian dwellings. Here the interior of a building is represented divided into four distinct compartments, and exhibiting various people at their several household duties. We have even a glimpse at an Assyrian groom, who, in an adjoining building, is cleaning a horse. Prisoners are introduced even here, in this domestic scene, conducted by a warrior to an eunuch; and in the distance are soldiers, with lions' skins, dancing to the vibrations of a guitar. The second slab is a continuation of the first. Here men are mounted in war chariots, while others holding the heads of their enemies in their hands are on foot: and a bird, grasping in its claws a human head, soars above. That slab marked 3, and placed against the window hereabouts, was extracted from the centre of the great mound of Nimroud. Here camels, preceded by a woman, are pourtrayed. The slab marked 5 bears the representation of an Assyrian divinity, with four wings, the head surmounted by the conical cap with two horns, and the left hand holding a circlet of beads. A winged figure occurs also on the sixth slab of this compartment, holding a bearded ear of corn in one hand, and a goat in the other. The slabs of the ninth compartment have also representations of winged figures. The fourth, with the eagle head, and holding a fir-cone and a basket. This figure is thus described by Mr. Layard: "A human body, clothed in robes similar to those of the winged men already described, was surmounted by the head of an eagle or of a vulture. The curved beak, of considerable length, was half open, and displayed a narrow-pointed tongue, on which were still the remains of red paint. On the shoulders fell the usual curled and bushy hair of the Assyrian images, and a comb of feathers rose on the top of the head. Two wings sprang from the back, and in either hand was the square vessel and fir-cone. In a kind of girdle were three daggers, the handle of one being in the form of the head of a bull. They may have been of precious metal, but more probably of copper, inlaid with ivory or enamel, as a few days before a copper dagger-handle, precisely similar in form to one of those carried by this figure, hollowed to receive an ornament of some such material, had been discovered in the S.W. ruins, and is now preserved in the British Museum. This effigy, which probably typified by its mythic form the union of certain divine attributes, may perhaps be identified with the god Nisroch, in whose temple Sennacherib was slain by his sons after his return from his unsuccessful expedition against Jerusalem; the word Nisr signifying, in all Semitic languages, 'an eagle.'" The slabs arranged in the tenth compartment are interesting. On the first, two horsemen, whose peaked helmets suggest that they are Assyrians, are charging another horseman with their spears. Behind is a bird carrying off the entrails of the killed. The second slab, covered with an inscription, formed part of the northwest palace. Winged figures are traceable on other slabs in this compartment; and in the centre the visitor should remark the only Assyrian statue yet discovered. It is a seated figure, headless. Between the tenth and eleventh compartments are placed some painted bricks, used in adorning the interior of Assyrian edifices. The eleventh and last compartment contains two slabs, on the first of which is a monarch holding two arrows in token of peace. Having fully examined these objects, the visitor has done with the Nimroud room. Of the romantic stories connected with the researches for the invaluable fragments it contains, we should be glad to give the reader a faint sketch. How Mr. Layard struggled against all kinds of difficulties; slept in hovels not sheltered from the rain; used his table as his roof by night; rode backwards and forwards from Nimroud to Mosul to expostulate with the vexatious interferences of a tyrannical old pasha; cheered the labours of his superstitious workmen; celebrated the discovery of certain remains with substantial feastings and music: made peace with a wandering Arab who threatened to rob him: these, and a thousand other adventures, recorded in his narrative of his discoveries, give an additional zest to the curiosity with which visitors enter this Nimroud room.

And now the visitor may make his way back to the great entrance-hall of the Museum, where his third visit should close. In the hall are deposited four colossal specimens of sculpture from Nimroud. The first of these, to which the visitor should direct his attention, is a colossal figure of a winged human-headed bull, found by Mr. Layard at the portal of a door at Nimroud. Of the discovery of this marvellous specimen of ancient Assyrian art, Mr. Layard gives a graphic account:--"I was returning to the mound, when I saw two Arabs urging their mares to the top of their speed. On approaching me, they stopped. 'Hasten, O Bey!' exclaimed one of them, 'hasten to the diggers; for they have found Nimrod himself. Wallah! it is wonderful, but it is true! we have seen him with our eyes. There is no god but God!' and both joining in this pious exclamation, they galloped off, without further words, in the direction of their tents. On reaching the ruins I descended into the new trench, and found the workmen, who had already seen me as I approached, standing near a heap of baskets and cloaks. Whilst Awad advanced and asked for a present to celebrate the occasion, the Arabs withdrew the screen they had hastily constructed, and disclosed an enormous human head, sculptured in full out of the alabaster of the country. They had uncovered the upper part of a figure, the remainder of which was still buried in the earth. I saw at once that the head must belong to a winged lion or bull, similar to those of Khorsabad and Persepolis. It was in admirable preservation. The expression was calm, yet majestic; and the outline of the features showed a freedom and knowledge of art scarcely to be looked for in works of so remote a period. I was not surprised that the Arabs had been amazed and terrified at this apparition. It required no stretch of imagination to conjure up the most strange fancies. This gigantic head, blanched with age, thus rising from the bowels of the earth, might well have belonged to one of those fearful beings which are pictured in the traditions of the country as appearing to mortals, slowly ascending from the regions below. One of the workmen, on catching the first glimpse of the monster, had thrown down his basket, and had run off towards Mosul as fast as his legs could carry him." The marvellous fidelity and power with which this, and the colossal human-headed bull are executed, must astonish the most uninstructed observer. For an account of the marvellous labour at the cost of which these colossal Assyrian works were conveyed from Asia Minor to the British Museum, we must refer the reader to Mr. Layard's excellent condensed account of his researches, published by Mr. Murray. And with the contemplation of these mysterious monuments of the past, the visitor should close his third visit to the national Museum.

He may usefully recapitulate the points of his present visit. He has been travelling for hours amongst the wrecks of the remote past. Over vast tracts of land, where now the Turk lazily dreams away the hours, or moves only to destroy the remains of the ancient civilisation of his Asiatic provinces. Throughout this, his third visit, the visitor has been exploring the revelations of the past, written upon the face of Turkish provinces. The bigotry with which the explorers of Thebes, Nimroud, and Xanthus had to contend, is written in their histories of their labours. How when the human-headed bull was disclosed by the pick-axes of the Chaldaeans, the Arabs scampered off, and how all the natives thought that Nimroud himself--the mighty hunter--was rising grimly from the earth, are points in the discovery of this treasure which all should read. The vigour with which English and French explorers have possessed themselves of the treasures of ancient Egypt, the masterpieces from the Parthenon, the strange stone revelations of Lycia, and the majestic colossi of ancient Assyria, contrasts forcibly with the indolence of the Turk, who sat at hand to wonder at the enthusiasm of his Christian visitors. No more pitiful exhibition of a national character could be furnished by any passage in the history of the world than that which describes the ignorant and superstitious Turk grinding the sculpture of the Parthenon into mortar for his dwelling house. Truly, in all respects, is this a matter to be pondered by the general visitor, as he retreats from the national Museum for the third time. He has not passed an idle day here, wandering amid sphinxes, and tombs, and temples, and ancient gods. From the confusion he may gather something that shall not be altogether a useless subject for reflection as he wanders homewards. He may link himself with the remote past, recognise the elements of modern society in these stone revelations of the remote history of the world, feel the vibration of the great human heart coming to him even from the bowels of Egypt's pyramids. There he has their family histories written on their tombstones by weeping relatives; their religion, with all its debasing idolatry, strong in death, exhibiting pleasantly the firmness of their faith; splendid sarcophagi tardily wrought from massive rock, yet perseveringly accomplished in the strong conviction that the dead would shake off the mummy bandages, discharge the natron from their pores, reclaim their scattered intestines, pass the brain back through the nose into the skull, and once more feel quickening blood in the veins. Proudly men of the passing century look back upon all this worship of animals, upon the Egyptian Anubis, and the intestine genii with their animal heads; but even here, in this field of speculation, where the historian's hand wanders unsteadily about his page, and all wears a mythical air, pulses of human emotion are felt that assure us of the remote past. Strange that the chief chapters of ancient Egypt's history should have been written for moderns by her undertakers!

END OF THIRD VISIT.

VISIT THE FOURTH.

The visitor will now enter the museum to complete his inspection of its contents. His way lies once more to the west on entering the great hall, into the first Sculpture Gallery, or that which he will recognise as leading into the great central saloon. Here, as he pauses on the threshold of a noble room filled with splendid specimens of Greek art, he may recur to the historical points which these works illustrate. Throughout this, his last visit, he will be occupied with the examination of the works of the ancient Greeks. These works, as he will notice, are of various degrees of excellence. Already has he examined the rude labours of the Greek sculptors of Xanthus; and to-day his journey will be amid those more modern and perfect labours, performed when the talent of the Greeks was chiefly concentrated upon European ground. Although these glories of remote antiquity are here mostly in an admirable state of preservation, historians are generally lost in contradictions when they attempt to point to any particular piece of statuary as the labour of any known sculptor. The sculptor of the Venus de Medici is not known; and the Apollo Belvedere is a masterpiece, the author of which lies shrouded in the depths of the past. Rude and harsh were the early performances of the Greeks. We have histories of Greek sculptors who flourished many hundred years before our era; and of these the mythical Daedalus is the oldest and most renowned. This sculptor is reported to have flourished fourteen centuries before the Christian era. He is said to have fashioned colossal wooden statues; and Pausanias mentions his statue of Hercules in the possession of the Thebans, and his wooden Venus in the possession of the Delians. His Hercules, however, appears to have been considered his masterpiece; and Flaxman, commenting upon the antiquity of the figures of Hercules found on some coins, seems to think that we may not unreasonably conjecture that these are copies from the masterpiece of Daedalus. Other sculptors of the same name, appear to have flourished in the Achaic period of Grecian history. Indeed it is shrewdly conjectured that Daedalus derived his name from wooden statues called Daedala; and that amongst the ancient Greeks, Daedalus meant nothing more than one skilled in making Daedala. The earliest sculptures of the Greeks were fashioned of materials easily worked, as plaster, clay, and wood. Later they worked ivory, and began to understand the value of metals in statuary; and about five centuries before the Christian era, marble was used by sculptors for detached figures. In the infancy of Greek art, when sculptors were gradually acquiring the skill to fashion their creations out of the most durable material, many combinations of wood, stone, and metal were used, which would sadly shock the modern sculptor's eye;--wooden figures burnished with gold, and with painted vermilion faces, were fashioned in the age of Phidias; and it is believed by some, that this immortal sculptor helped to produce a statue of Jupiter, the face of which was of ivory and gold, and the body of gypsum and clay. Phidias may be fairly acknowledged as the first great Greek sculptor, of whose career and whose works we have indisputable accounts. He founded, and represents all the excellencies of the highest school of Greek art. The sculptors who came after him, as Lysippus the favourite of the great Alexander, paid greater regard to graces of detail and to finish; but of those sublime effects, those forms of gods in human shape which really impress the modern spectator with their almost superhuman beauty, Phidias was the creator. The sculptures known to the public as the Townley collection, are sculptures generally of a more modern date than those in the Elgin and Phigaleian Saloons. The collection has undoubtedly many specimens of the rudest eras of Greek art: but its most striking groups, to the general visitor, will be undoubtedly those finished statues and compositions which represent the ages when Greece was a great European power, and that subsequent period when the Greek sculptors plied their chisels under the patronage of Roman conquerors. In this room the visitor will once more remark, how large a proportion of these priceless relics have been gleaned from ancient sepulchres. Even as he enters the room, he may perceive on the right, the front of a tomb from Athens, carved in high relief; and on the left, the front of another tomb, also sculptured, from Delos.

The room is divided into compartments which the visitor should examine in their regular order of rotation. He will begin therefore, of course with the

FIRST DIVISION.

Before the first pilaster let the visitor notice at once a small seated statue of Cybele or Fortune, from Athens, presented to the nation by J.S. Gaskoin, Esq. Other remarkable objects to be examined before the visitor fixes his attention upon the contents of the case deposited here, are a bust of Demosthenes; a sepulchral altar or cippus, ornamented with sphinxes, etc.; and a sepulchral stele, inscribed with the name of the son of Artemidorus, who is reclining upon a couch, and crowning himself. Over the case are deposited the end of a sarcophagus ornamented with a Bacchus reclining on a satyr; a bust of Julius Caesar; a sepulchral cippus; and a Greek stele. On the case are a head found near Rome, probably of Mercury: and the bust of a Muse crowned with a laurel wreath.

Having examined these objects, the visitor should occupy himself with the contents of the case. Here are some beautiful specimens of Greek art--some mere fragments, others in a wonderful state of preservation. Here are one of those funeral masks anciently used to cover the face of a corpse; the votive mask of a bearded satyr; a votive patera with bas-reliefs representing Silenus and a satyr, another with the head of a bearded Bacchus, and a panther; various heads of Hercules; a Venus attended by two Cupids; a bust of Vitellius; a head of Vulcan; a bust of Caracalla; a head of Juno; a head of the daughter of Titus, Julia; a mutilated figure, about the neck of which a scarabaeus is suspended; the torso of a satyr; a variety of fragments, here an arm holding a butterfly--there two lions' paws--there a gladiator's foot--there the fragment of a serpent. Having noticed these scraps of ancient art, the visitor may direct his attention to the lower shelf, where he will observe some beautiful busts. These include one supposed to be of Sappho; a Minerva with a Corinthian helmet found at Rome; Bacchus; Apollo; a Parian marble bust of Diana from Rome; a queenly Juno wearing the splendone; terminal busts, joined back to back, of Hercules and Omphale. The upper shelf now remains for inspection. Here are three sepulchral tablets, and the fronts of two sarcophagi. The tablet from Crete, within a wreath, contains an inscription descriptive of honour conferred by the inhabitants of Crete upon an individual named Alexander, the gift to him being a golden crown. Having noticed the gay Cupids enacting Bacchanalians upon the first front of a sarcophagus, the visitor should pass on at once to the

SECOND DIVISION.

Here, in front of the pilaster, the visitor should remark a curious square altar, with Silvanus, to whom the altar is dedicated by the farm servant of Caius Coelius Heliodorus, Callistus; and a trophy discovered on the plains of Marathon.

Grouped in this division, are some fine works. First let the visitor remark two white marble Victories discovered in the ruins of the villa of Antoninus Pius, at Monte Cagnuolo. The first Victory is kneeling upon a bull which she is about to sacrifice; and the second also is kneeling upon, and about to stab, a bull. Then a fine bust of a laughing satyr will arrest the attention of the visitor; then a colossal foot in a sandal, under the front of a sarcophagus; then the votive torso, supposed to be that of an Athelete; then a red marble swan found in a vineyard near the Villa Pinciana; then a terminal statue of a satyr; then a bust of Diogenes; then a bust, conjectured to be part of the figure of a dying Amazon; then a bust of Atys. Turning to the upper shelf of this division, the visitor should notice the front and ends of a sarcophagus deposited there. Upon these Bacchus and Ariadne are represented in a chariot, heralded by Bacchanals, and drawn by Centaurs; and in other parts Pan is being castigated by a satyr, and carried off by two Cupids aided by a satyr. Turning to the lower shelf the visitor should examine several antique busts. First there is a bust, conjectured to be that of Achilles; then there is an old Hercules; then a Bacchante; then a bust of Aratus; a female head; and a tragic mask from the lid of a sarcophagus. With the examination of this shelf the visitor closes his inspection of the second division, and should at once advance into the

THIRD DIVISION.

First, let the visitor notice, placed in front of the third pilaster, a celebrated copy of the statue of Praxiteles, of Cupid bending his bow. This celebrated copy is four feet, three and a half inches, in height. It arrived in this country originally as a present to Edmund Burke, from Rome, by Barry, the painter. Numerous copies of this Cupid exist, and the one before the visitor is not the best.

In this compartment or division, the visitor should also remark several sepulchral urns with figures in relief. Amid other sepulchral monuments are, an altar inscribed by Annia Augustalis, to the manes of M. Clodius, his brother Felix, and to Tyrannus; and a bas-relief discovered near the mausoleum of Augustus, representing a Muse standing before a dramatic poet. Hereabouts also the visitor should notice an altar, ornamented with bas-reliefs, dedicated by Aurelius Timotheus to Diana; a small figure of Neptune from Athens; a veiled Ceres bearing a torch, from Athens; a draped Muse in terra cotta holding a lyre; and a cippus, with a representation of Silenus riding a panther. On turning to the lower shelf, the visitor will at once be struck with the sarcophagi. Here are three Etruscan sarcophagi, two of alabaster, and one in peperino. On all three are recumbent female figures, and in front of the first the hunt of the Calydonian boar; of the second, Scylla; and of the third, a bas-relief representing Achilles dragging Penthesilea from her chariot. On this shelf also are, a bas-relief showing Luna encompassed by the signs of the Zodiac, and a sun-dial supported by the claws and heads of lions. Turning now to the upper shelf, the visitor should examine the bas-reliefs deposited thereon. Upon the first, the visitor will notice a funeral car, shaped like a temple drawn by four horses, with Jupiter and the Dioscuri on the sides of the car; upon the second, the bas-relief represents Ulysses and Diomedes detecting Achilles disguised as a female among the daughters of Lycomedes; and the subject of the third relief is a marriage in the presence of Juno Pronuba, showing the bridegroom taking the bride's hand, and holding the marriage contract. Having glanced at these objects, the visitor's way lies forward to the

FOURTH DIVISION.

Here, in front of the pilaster, the visitor must at once examine the torso of a statue, supposed to be of Mercury; and a curious Greek circular altar, ornamented with the heads and fillets of bulls and stags, and inscribed with the names of Agathemeris and her son Sosicles of Tlos. Having examined these two prominently placed objects, the visitor should proceed at once to the general contents of the division. He will be probably attracted first to two terminal statues; or statues, of which the lower parts are not developed. They occur frequently among the remains of Greek sculpture. These terminal statues were held in great veneration; and they were found placed at the corners of streets, at the doors of private dwellings, and before temples. The custom of representing Mercury with a head upon a plain column, appears to have been the origin of a fashion which the Greeks subsequently extended to their representations of other deities. The terminal figure in this division, with the winged cap, illustrates the generality of these Hermae; it was found near Frascati, in the year 1770. The next remarkable object thàt will probably attract the visitor's attention is the figure, found at Rome, of an Egyptian tumbler, going through his performances on the back of a tame crocodile, a barbarous species of entertainment undoubtedly, but not more repulsive than that of the French aeroenaut of last year, floating over Paris on the back of an ostrich. Hereabouts are placed also a small statue of the three-fold Hecate, a Diana found in the Giustiniani Palace at Rome; a bust of Jupiter, conjectured to be a copy from the work of the celebrated sculptor Polycletus, and a sphinx. Here, too, are some interesting bas-reliefs. Upon one a Bacchante (supposed to be a copy from Scopas), is represented with a knife in her hand, and holding part of a kid; upon another (part of a sarcophagus), Priam is represented praying to Achilles to give up Hector's body; upon a third (a cippus) birds are drinking; and upon a fourth (a fountain) are Pans and satyrs. Before turning to the lower shelf, the visitor should also notice in this neighbourhood a beautiful group of two dogs, found on the Monte Cagnuolo; a votive foot, with a coiling serpent, and one or two sepulcral urns with inscriptions. Upon the lower shelf are deposited an interesting series of busts, including one of the Emperor Septimius Severus, found on the Palatine Hill; one of Hadrian, found at Tivoli, on the site of Hadrian's Villa; one from Athens, of the Emperor Nero; and one of Caracalla, found in the Nunnery Gardens at the Quatro Fontane, on the Esquiline Hill. Upon the upper shelf are two busts in relief, and the front of a sarcophagus, with elaborate representations of the Muses. Here is Terpsichore with the lyre of dancing, Thalia with the mask of comedy. And now the way lies once more forward, into the

FIFTH DIVISION.

Before the fifth pilaster is a notable piece of sculpture found in the villa of Antoninus Pius--an erect figure of the youthful Bacchus clothed in the skin of a panther; and here also is a square altar ornamented with sphinxes in bas-relief, Apollo, Diana, and various religious symbols. A colossal toe attracts considerable attention in this division. It may have been an ornament in the rooms of an Eisenberg of the ancients, but more probably has been lost by a god. Let the visitor pause here before the terminal bust of Aeschines the orator, who impeached Demosthenes out of jealousy for his popularity with the people of Athens, and sullenly retired, after losing his cause and being mulcted of a thousand drachmas as the accuser, to Rhodes, where he occupied himself in teaching rhetoric. Other terminal statues occur in this division. Among these, in a glass, are small terminal busts, joined back to back, of Bacchus and Libera; three yellow and red marble heads of Libera; a yellow marble bearded Bacchus; and the bust of a Greek poet discovered at Bitolia. Hereabouts also are, a female head, the eyes of which have traces of inlaying; a bas-relief of Antinous; a curious female head, with the hair of a distinct block of marble, fitted upon it; the head of a child from Rome; the head of Jupiter from the corner of a sarcophagus; busts of Hercules and Serapis; a remarkable altar in the Egyptian style, curiously carved with the bull Apis, and Harpocrates drawn in a car by a hippopotamus. Turning to the upper shelf, the visitor will notice a satyr playing on a flute; six Amazons carved upon the fragment of a sarcophagus; and a sarcophagus found at Tusculum, with representations of Cupids bearing away the arms of Mars. A series of busts are deposited upon the lower shelf. These include busts of the wife of the Emperor Domitian; bust of Olympia; bust of the wife of Hadrian, Julia Sabina; bust of Tiberius; and a bust of Augustus. Before leaving this room the visitor should not fail to notice a few antiquities which should particularly interest him. These form a group of relics found in this country. They illustrate the doings of the Romans in this country.

ANTIQUITIES OF BRITAIN.

The first of these objects which the visitor will remark, is a curious cylindrical sarcophagus, discovered in the neighbourhood of St. Alban's, so lately as the year 1831. It contained some Roman vases. Another sarcophagus found at Southfleet, in Kent, is also included in the collection. In this sarcophagus several interesting relics were discovered, including a vessel containing burnt bones; and purple leather shoes embroidered with gold, and in the same neighbourhood other relics, including an earthern vessel, also containing bones, were found. The next object to which the visitor should direct his attention is the old cistern of a blacksmith, which had been found at Chesterford, in Essex, which turned out to be an ancient relic sculptured in high relief with figures of Jupiter, Mercury, Mars, and Venus. Three or four Roman altars found in various parts of the country, one to AEsculapius; a bas-relief of a Roman standard of the second legion; and pigs of lead inscribed with the names of Roman emperors. Having examined these objects, the visitor should pass at once westward into the

PHIGALEIAN SALOON.

He may here take a seat for a few moments and read the points of history which belong to this saloon, before he commences his examination of it. One year, while the present century was young, fifteen gentlemen encamped round about the ruins of a temple, known to the neighbouring inhabitants as the "columns." These columns were those believed to be the ruins of a temple of Apollo Epicurius, built by the citizens of ancient Phigaleia, in Arcadia. These "columns" were situated upon a shelf of land, high up the side of Mount Cotilium, and surrounded by a rich and various landscape. Lying scattered about were the shattered fragments of the sculptured frieze of the temple; and, with infinite labour the camp of explorers succeeded in gathering together and arranging the slabs which are now deposited in this, the Phigaleian saloon. To the sound of Arcadian music, workmen excavated in the neighbourhood of these ruins; and in 1814 the Prince Regent obtained a grant of 15,000L. to purchase them for the British Museum.

The subjects represented by these sculptures are, the battle of the Centaurs and the Lapithae, and the war between the Amazons and Athenians--mythical struggles upon which Greek sculptors were fond of exercising their imagination. THE BATTLE OF THE CENTAURS is the first to which the visitor should direct his attention. The origin of this myth is thus described by Sir Henry Ellis: "The story of the Centaurs, it is remarked, is of Thessalian origin. The people of Thessaly were remarkably expert in horsemanship, and were supposed to be the first in Greece who practised the art of riding on horseback. Pelion, and other mountains in this part of Greece, abounding in wild bulls, these ferocious animals were frequently hunted by the people of the country on horseback, and when overtaken were seized by their pursuers, who caught hold of them by the horns, in a manner not less dexterous than daring. Hence, these hunters acquired the name of Centauri and Hippocentauri. The novel sight of a man seated on a horse, and galloping over the plains with more than human velocity, might easily suggest to the minds of an ignorant peasantry, the idea of an animal composed partly of a man and partly of a horse; and it was from this simple origin, according to some explanations, that the fable of the Centaurs sprung. We must remark, that we place no confidence in the proposed etymology of the word Centauros, and almost as little in the explanation of the story. The centaur Chiron in Homer was a model of justice, and the poet appears to have had no idea of the monstrous combination of two animals. Pindar, in his second Pythian Ode, first makes us acquainted with the Hippocentaur, or half horse and half man. Though it cannot be imagined that the Greeks ever regarded this tradition otherwise than as a fable, so far as the double nature of the animal was concerned, yet it is curious, to observe, with what care and devotion they recorded the particulars of this fiction in their poems, sculpture, paintings, and other monuments of art. The Centaurs were invited to the nuptials of Pirithous, king of the Lapithae. During the marriage feast, one of the Centaurs, named Eurytion, or Eurytus, with the characteristic brutality of his nature, and elated by the effects of wine, offered violence to the person of Hippodamia, the bride. This outrageous act was immediately resented by Theseus, the friend of Pirhitous, who hurled a large vessel of wine at the head of the offender, which brought him lifeless to the ground. A general engagement then ensued between the two parties; and the Centaurs not only sought to revenge the death of their companion, Eurytus, but likewise attempted to carry off the females who were guests at the nuptials. In this conflict, sustained on both sides with great fury, the Centaurs were finally vanquished, and driven out of Thessaly; after which they took up their abode in Arcadia, where they provoked the anger of Hercules, who completely destroyed the whole of their race. Such is the general outline of the mythic history of the Centaurs."

Bearing this outline of the classical story in his mind, the visitor may at once proceed to examine the first eleven slabs upon which the incidents in the story of the Centaurs and the Lapithae are elaborated. The visitor will, of course, begin with tablet No. 1, and proceed to the others in the regular order in which they are marked.

On approaching the first slab (1) the visitor will perceive a Centaur overcome by two Lapithae, and about to be dispatched. Another Centaur from behind, however, arrests the uplifted arm of one Lapitha. The battle proceeds fiercely on the second slab (2). A Centaur is tearing the shoulder of a Lapitha with his teeth, while the Lapitha drives a stout sword direct into his assailant's body. A dead Centaur lies in the foreground, and the heels of the stabbed Centaur strike against the shield of a second Lapitha. The origin of the battle begins to appear on the third slab (3), where a woman is represented with a child in her arms resisting the violence of a Centaur, while another Centaur at the further end of the slab is getting the better of a kneeling Lapitha. The fourth tablet would be probably unintelligible to the general visitor without special explanation. Here the Centaurs are endeavouring to crush an enemy with huge blocks of stone. This particular enemy is the Caeneus of Greek fable, whom Neptune had rendered invulnerable to the effect of swords and clubs, and whom Centaurs are endeavouring to overcome by crushing his body with masses of rock. The fifth slab (5) presents a more cheerful view of the battle for the Lapithae; here two Centaurs are being overcome by two of their enemies in revenge for their brutal conduct at the bridal banquet. The sixth tablet (6) again illustrates the hazards of war. Here a female is between two of the brutal Centaurs, one of whom has felled a Lapitha to the ground; but the left hand part of the slab is so mutilated that the merits of the sculpture are here hardly appreciable. The seventh (7) slab also represents the Lapithae losing ground. Here, it has been shrewdly conjectured the chief personages of the battle are represented. The female in the arms of the Centaur is supposed to be Hippodamia; and the figure struggling from the grasp of another Centaur, that of King Pirithous fighting for his outraged bride. The next tablet (8) is in a very dilapidated condition. The central figure is that of a muscular Centaur, with his mantle flowing from his neck, in the act of hurling something at a Lapitha who stands stoutly on the defensive, while in the further corner a female with her child is flying from pursuers. The ninth tablet (9) discovers two vanquished Centaurs, and Lapithae in the act of dispatching their mongrel enemies. The battle is represented at its climax on the next slab (10). Here, as the wicked Centaur, Eurytion, is disrobing the King's bride, and her bridesmaid is indulging in exaggerated attitudes of despair, a figure supposed to be that of the renowned founder of Athens, Theseus, springs upon the Centaur's shoulders, and drags back his head, that the brute may not gaze upon the charms he would pollute. The figure behind the bride is supposed to represent Diana, the goddess of Chastity. It is a pity that the leg and arm of the Theseus, and one arm of the bridesmaid are fractured. The last slab of those sculptured with the battle of the Centaurs, represents Apollo and Diana in a car--Apollo the deliverer; Diana the guardian of female chastity. Having fully examined these beautiful specimens of Greek art of the time of Pericles, the visitor should turn at once to the remaining slabs, which are devoted to the illustration of

A BATTLE WITH THE AMAZONS.

Plutarch gives a graphic account of those dissensions between Theseus and the Amazons, which terminated in the famous war here celebrated. "Philochorus," he says, "and some others relate, that he (Theseus) sailed in company with Hercules into the Euxine Sea, to wage war with the Amazons, and that he received Antiope as the reward of his valour, but the greater number, (among whom are Pherecydes, Hellanicus, and Herodotus,) tell us, that Theseus made the voyage with his own fleet alone, some time after Hercules, and took that Amazon captive, which is indeed the more probable account; for we do not read that any other of his fellow-warriors made any Amazon prisoner. But Bion says, he took and carried her off by a stratagem. The Amazons (he informs us) being naturally lovers of men, were so far from avoiding Theseus when he touched upon their coasts, that they sent him presents. Theseus invited Antiope, who brought them, into his ship, and, as soon as she was aboard, set sail. But the account of one Menecrates, who published a history of Nice in Bithynia, is that Theseus, having Antiope aboard his vessel, remained in those parts some time; and that he was attended in this expedition by three young men of Athens, who were brothers, Enneos, Thoas, and Solon. The last of these, unknown to the rest, fell in love with Antiope, and communicated his passion to one of his companions, who applied to Antiope about the affair. She firmly rejected his pretensions, but treated him with civility, and prudently concealed the matter from Theseus. But Solon, in despair, having leaped into a river and drowned himself, Theseus, then sensible of the cause, and the young man's passion, lamented his fate, and in his sorrow recollected an order of the priestess, which he had formerly received at Delphi; that when, in some foreign country, he should labour under the greatest affliction, he should build a city there, and leave some of his followers to govern it. Hence, he called the city which he built Pythopolis, after the Pythian god, and the neighbouring river, in honour of the young man, Solon. He left the two surviving brothers to govern it, and give it laws; and along with them Hermus, who was of one of the best families in Athens. From him the inhabitants of Pythopolis call a certain place in their city Hermus's House, and, by exchanging an accent, transfer the honour from the hero to the god (Mercury). Hence the war with the Amazons took its rise: and it appears to have been no slight or womanish enterprise, for they could not have encamped in the town, or joined battle on the ground about the Pnyx and the Museum, or fallen in so intrepid a manner upon the city of Athens, unless they had first reduced the country about it. It is difficult, indeed, to believe (though the story is told by Hellanicus) that they crossed the Cimmerian Bosphorus upon the ice, but that they encamped almost in the heart of the city, is confirmed by the names of places, and by the tombs of those that perished there." The Amazons, according to fabulous history, were a warlike race of women, who reared only their female children, and lived as a nation apart from the male sex. They are said to have founded many cities in Asia Minor, to have been expert horsewomen, and to have amputated their left breast the more easily to use their bows. Greek sculptors delighted to avail themselves of this mythic war between men and women, in which the heroes do not appear to have used their weapons lightly, in consideration of the sex of their opponents. The splendid group by Kiss, casts of which are now in many English homes, shows that the capacity to deal with the classic subject has not altogether faded from the world. The Amazons themselves bid fair to accomplish a resurrection across the Atlantic. Rumours reach us here in England of female societies associated to make war upon the tyranny of the opposite sex, and to adopt certain eccentricities of costume. It is not improbable that these agitators will soon constitute themselves into a distinct nation, and defy the valour of the masculine Yankee.

The visitor, on turning, thus far informed, to the slabs upon which the war with the Amazons is represented, will notice that these mythic females present no appearance of the rumoured amputation. The weapons that should be in the hands of most of the figures are lost, but it is believed that they were of bronze, and the holes by which they were fastened to the hands of the figures may yet be traced. On presenting himself before the first slab (12), the visitor will see the figure of an Athenian dragging an Amazon to the ground by her hair, while another Amazon is protecting a fallen sister in the corner. This scene will shock the gallantry of the unprepared visitor, who should, nevertheless, compose himself to explain to his partner the kind of women with whom the Athenians had to deal. The second slab (13), represents a wounded Amazon sinking to the earth, and an Athenian and an Amazon in full combat, but upon the third (14), the visitor will remark the havoc which the Amazons could make. Here, on the right, an Athenian protecting himself from attack with his shield, is leading a wounded man from the field, and to the right a male figure is bearing off a body, from which a central Amazon is snatching a shield. On the next slab (15), two Amazons are engaged with two Athenians. To the left, where the head of the vanquished Amazon remains, the slab is much injured; but to the right the Athenian felled by the Amazon is clearly distinguishable. A wounded Athenian lies in the left corner of the next slab (16), supported by a companion; while another Athenian is endeavouring to beat off a lusty Amazon, who appears determined to fight for every inch of the ground. For the first time an Amazon occurs on horseback on the next slab (17). Here a sturdy Athenian is dragging her from her seat, while another Amazon is warding off a blow, and preparing to strike one at the same time, in the right corner. The central figure of the next slab (18), (the longest in the collection,) is the hero Theseus, recognisable by the lion's skin about him, the huge paw of which lies against his left leg. Theseus, who is about to deal a deadly blow at a mounted Amazon (whose body is effaced), is prevented by an interposing Amazon, while an Athenian, who is trampled upon by the horse, is preparing to do severe work with his sword. To the right, an Athenian is unceremoniously removing a wounded Amazon from her fallen horse. The next group (19) represents two couples fighting: an Athenian, protected by a helmet and cuirass, has thrown an Amazon, and on the right of the slab an Amazon has thrown an Athenian. The next slab (20) is severely mutilated; but an Amazon attending to a wounded companion, and others fighting in the left corner are distinguishable. The next tablet represents two Athenians and two Amazons; the central figure (an Athenian) has his foot upon the knee of a fallen Amazon, who appears to be asking mercy. The last slab but one (22) represents an Athenian dragging an Amazon from an altar, while to the right an Amazon is vigorously assailing another Athenian. Upon the last slab (23) are four Amazons and one wounded Athenian, who is endeavouring to ward off an impending blow from the central figure. Having noticed these slabs, the wondrous workmanship of which must surprise the most indifferent and ill-informed observer, the visitor should at once turn to the other fragments arranged and numbered in the saloon. The fragments marked successively from 24 to 40, are parts of the temple to Apollo, from which the Phigaleian slabs were taken. Having cursorily examined these, the visitor should at once turn to the fragment of a bas-relief, marked 41, which properly belongs to the Elgin collection. Here Hercules is represented holding Diomed, King of Thrace, by the head, and is about to strike him. Further on are some interesting relics, collected by Colonel Leake. First, there is a headless female statue, draped, from Sparta (43); then the torso of a naked Apollo from the Peloponnese; then a small, shattered Hercules, without head, arms, or feet, found on the coast of Laconia. Proceeding with his examination of the miscellaneous objects in the saloon, he may notice successively, the head of Jupiter, from Phrygia (47); a curious sepulchral inscription from Halicarnassus (48), forbidding any one, except relations, from occupying the tomb to which it belonged; a bas-relief from Thessaly (51) representing a dedication of hair to Poseidon: an alto-relievo torso of Triton (56); and the pedestal of the statue of Jupiter Urius (55), which stood in the temple of that god, at the mouth of the Euxine.

Directing his attention to the fragments which occupy the wall space below the Phigaleian frieze, he will find eleven fine bas-reliefs from the celebrated tomb erected at Halicarnassus, in the year 353 B.C., in honour of Mausolus, King of Caria, by Artemisia, his wife. Here the power of the later Greek sculptors is employed upon the battles of the Athenians with the Amazons. Above the Phigaleian frieze, against the walls are placed two pediments, copied from those which ornamented the western and eastern ends of the temple of Jupiter Panhellenius, in AEgina.

Among the miscellaneous fragments in the saloon, the visitor has yet to notice a fine torso of a nude Venus; a statue of Discobolus, who is throwing a quoit, found in Hadrian's Villa Tiburtina; part of a statue of Hymen; and at the ends of the saloon the visitor should notice some specimens from the old temple of Selinus, which are valued as probably representing some of the earliest extant specimens of Greek art. Among the subjects represented are Perseus killing the Gorgon Medusa, and Hercules and the Cecrops. Having examined these objects, the visitor has brought his examination of the Phigaleian Saloon to a close, and he should forthwith enter upon the great labour of his fourth visit, by proceeding to the west into the noble room devoted to the

ELGIN MARBLES.

These marbles have become celebrated throughout the civilised world, and the name of Elgin is inseparably connected henceforth with the finest extant specimens of the power of Phidias. The artistic excellencies of these relics of a remote civilisation have been so frequently explained to the public, and their beauties are so generally felt, that it suffices to introduce the general visitor to the room, and to guide him about it, without bidding him halt to learn the estimation set upon these works by great art authorities. After he has received the natural impression which these works cannot fail to produce on his mind, he may wish to know something of the times and men which these represent; he may be glad to learn so much as is known of Phidias. No man even with the poorest sense of the beautiful can, we apprehend, wander about this saloon without being touched. Therefore we proceed at once to guide the visitor on his journey. But it is necessary that he should know something of the building, of which these fragments formed parts:--"The Parthenon," says Colonel Leake, "was constructed entirely of white marble, from Mount Pentelicus. It consisted of a cell, surrounded with a peristyle, which had eight Doric columns in the fronts, and seventeen in the sides. These forty-six columns were six feet two inches in diameter at the base, and thirty-four feet in height, standing upon a pavement, to which there was an ascent of three steps. The total height of the temple above its platform was about sixty-five feet. Within the peristyle at either end, there was an interior range of six columns, of five feet and a half in diameter, standing before the end of the cell, and forming a vestibule to its door. There was an ascent of two steps into these vestibules from the peristyle. The cell, which was sixty-two feet and a half broad within, was divided into two unequal chambers, of which the western was forty-three feet ten inches long, and the eastern ninety-eight feet seven inches. The ceiling of the former was supported by four columns, of about four feet in diameter, and that of the latter by sixteen columns of about three feet. It is not known of what order were the interior columns of either chamber. Those of the western having been thirty-six feet in height, their proportion must have been nearly the same as that of the Ionic columns of the vestibule of the Propylaea, whence it seems highly probable that the same order was used in the interior of both those contemporary buildings. In the eastern chamber of the Parthenon, the smallness of the diameter of the columns leaves little doubt that there was an upper range, as in the temples of Paestum and AEgina. It is to be lamented that no remains of any of them have been found, as they might have presented some new proofs of the taste and invention of the architects of the time of Pericles.

"Such was the simple construction of this magnificent building, which, by the united excellencies of materials, design, and decorations, was the most perfect ever executed. Its dimensions of two hundred and twenty-eight feet by a hundred and two, with a height of sixty-six feet to the top of the pediment, were sufficiently great to give an impression of grandeur and sublimity, which was not disturbed by any obtrusive subdivision of parts, such as is found to diminish the effects of some larger modern buildings, where the same singleness of design is not observed. In the Parthenon, whether viewed at a small or at a great distance, there was nothing to divert the spectator's contemplation from the simplicity and majesty of mass and outline, which forms the first and most remarkable object of admiration in a Greek temple; and it was not until the eye was satiated with the contemplation of the entire edifice, that the spectator was tempted to examine the decorations with which this building was so profusely adorned; for the statues of the pediments, the only decoration which was very conspicuous by its magnitude and position, being enclosed within frames, which formed an essential part of the design of either front, had no more obtrusive effect than an ornamented capital to a single column."

Bearing this outline of the building in mind, the visitor may at once proceed to examine the ruins of this fine monument of ancient genius, which are deposited in the Elgin Saloon of our National Museum. First, he may notice those alto-relievos, known as the

METOPES[9] OF THE PARTHENON.

The subject of these sculptures has been familiarised to the visitor in the Phigaleian marbles. Here, again, is the war of the Athenians, on behalf of the Lapithae, with the Centaurs, the sculptor's subject. On entering the room, the visitor will notice various numbers on each marble: THE RED NUMBERS are those to which we refer throughout.

The first metope to which the visitor will, in natural order, direct his attention, is that marked 1. Here an Athenian has his knee upon the back of a Centaur and one arm round his neck, while the other (which is broken off) was evidently represented raised to strike a fatal blow into the Centaur's body. The second metope (2) also represents an Athenian subduing a Centaur. This group is much injured, the head of the Athenian and that of the Centaur being missing; but the Athenian has his knee firmly planted upon his brutal enemy's hind quarters, and his arm (strongly developed) was evidently firmly clutching the Centaur's hair. The third metope (3) shows an Athenian under very disadvantageous circumstances. Here a Centaur is about to deal a tremendous blow with a wine vessel at the head of his crouching enemy, who is endeavouring to ward off its effects with his ample shield. The heads of these figures are casts from the originals, which are in the Royal Museum at Copenhagen. The fourth metope (4) has been so mutilated that the figure of the Athenian, which was once upon it, is wholly effaced, and the Centaur has the head, part of two legs, and both arms, wanting. Originally the Centaur was holding an Athenian by his hair. The fifth metope (5) is also much mutilated; but here both figures were evidently represented mutually confident of victory. A vigorous action is represented upon the sixth metope (6), where an Athenian is seizing a Centaur by the throat, while, with the right hand, he is prepared to deal a fatal stroke. The seventh metope (7) is much mutilated; but the figure of an Athenian thrown, and a Centaur trampling upon him, are clearly discernible. There is fine action in the eighth metope (8), where the Centaur has seized his adversary by the foot, and is hurling him backwards to the earth. Under the Athenian the visitor will notice a circular drinking vessel, indicative of the revel at which the cause of quarrel originated. The next metope (9) (or rather a cast from the metope in the Louvre at Paris) represents a Centaur in the act of seizing a female, who is resisting him: both heads are wanted. The drapery about the female is beautifully executed. Matters have arrived at a desperate pitch with the combatants represented on the tenth metope (10), where the Centaur, with starting eyes and uplifted arms, is about to strike a determined Athenian, who has planted his foot against the Centaur's breast, and is determined to do his work. The next metope (11) is a fine specimen of sculpture. Here an Athenian has seized a Centaur by the jaw, from behind. The drapery that falls from the fine form of the Greek is exquisitely folded, and the figure itself is finished with masterly skill. A victorious Centaur holding forth a mantle of lion's skin, is the central figure of the next metope (12). Below lies the dead body of an Athenian: all the muscles marked and rigid. It is supposed that the following metope (13) represents the Centaur Eurytion carrying off Hippodamia. The drapery of the female figure is exquisite. The fourteenth metope (14) represents an Athenian thrown by a Centaur. The Athenian, however, is not idle, having buried a weapon in the left side of his adversary, and attempting to seize a stone with his left hand. The fifteenth metope (15) represents a Centaur holding an Athenian; while the Athenian has revenged himself by planting that decisive kind of blow known in pugilistic circles as "a bruiser" upon the Centaur's cheek. This metope is more angular in execution than the other metopes; and was probably executed, under the guidance of Phidias, by one of the old school of Greek sculptors. The last, or sixteenth metope (16), is supposed to have been executed by the same inferior hand as that employed upon the fifteenth. Here the contest between the Centaur and the Athenian is undecided. Metope 16c has been recently discovered at Athens.

Having fully examined these fine specimens of Greek sculpture, the visitor may at once turn to other parts of the great temple, examining now and then, to guide his impressions, the restored model which stands near the south-east corner of the room. His business is now with the frieze that ran round the building behind the columns, and upon which a series of bas-reliefs were sculptured; of which Sir Henry Ellis gives the following clear outline:--

THE FRIEZE OF THE PARTHENON.

"One of the richest objects with which Phidias embellished the outside of the temple of the Parthenon, was, without doubt, that uninterrupted series of bas-reliefs which occupied the upper part of the walls within the colonnade, at the height of the frieze of the Pronaos, and which was continued entirely round the building. The situation afforded to the work only a secondary light, and, so far, prescribed to Phidias the manner in which he was to direct the execution of the figures.

"From the position intended for it, it was evident that the direct rays of the sun could never reach the Panathenaic frieze. Being placed immediately below the soffit, it received all its light from between the columns, and by reflection from the pavement below. The flatness of the sculpture is thus sufficiently accounted for; had the relief been prominent, the upper parts could not have been seen; the shade projected by the sculpture would have rendered it dark, and the parts would have been reduced by their shadows. The frieze could only be seen in an angle of forty-two degrees and a half.

"The subject represented the sacred procession which was celebrated every fifth year in honour of Minerva, the guardian goddess of the city, and embraced in its composition all the external observances of the highest festival of the Athenians.

"The blocks of marble of which the frieze was composed were three feet four inches high; they were placed about nine feet within the external row of columns; and occupied, slab after slab, a space of five hundred and twenty-four feet in length.

As a connected subject, this was the most extensive piece of sculpture ever made in Greece. The images of the gods, deified heroes, basket bearers, bearers of libatory vessels, trains of females, persons of every age and sex, men on horseback, victims, charioteers--in short, the whole people were represented in it conveying, in solemn pomp, to this very temple of the Parthenon, the sacred veil which was to be suspended before the statue of the goddess within.

"Meursius, in his Panathenaea and Reliquiae Atticae, has collected from ancient authors many particulars concerning this Peplus. It was the work of young virgins selected from the best families in Athens, over whom two of the principal, called Arrephorae, were superintendents. On it was embroidered the battle of the gods and giants; amongst the gods was Jupiter hurling his thunderbolts against the rebellious crew, and Minerva, seated in her chariot, appeared as the vanquisher of Typhon or Enceladus. In the Hecuba of Euripides, the chorus of captive Trojan females are lamenting, in anticipation, the evils which they will suffer in the land of the Greeks. 'In the city of Pallas, of Athena, on the beautiful seat in the woven peplus I shall yoke colts to a chariot, painting them in various different coloured threads, or else the races of the Titans, whom Zeus, the son of Kronos, puts to sleep in fiery all-surrounding flame.' The names of those Athenians who had been eminent for military virtue, were also embroidered on it. This will explain the following allusion in the Knights of Aristophanes, where the chorus says--'We wish to praise our fathers, because they were an honour to this country and worthy of the *peplus*: in battles by land and in the ship-girt armament conquering on all occasions they exalted this city.' When the festival was celebrated, this peplus was brought from the Acropolis, where it had been worked, down into the city; it was then displayed and suspended as a sail to the ship, which on that day, attended by a numerous and splendid procession, was conducted through the Ceramicus and other principal parts, till it had made the circuit of the Acropolis; it was then carried up to the Parthenon, and there consecrated to Minerva." This splendid series of sculptures forms the gem of the Elgin collection. The museum possesses no less than two hundred feet of the original frieze, in addition to upwards of seventy feet in casts. The wonderful variety, the perfect drawing, the classic grace, and the unity of conception displayed in this work, entitle it to rank as the most precious relic of antiquity saved to moderns from the wrecks of time. Starting from the left side of the entrance door to the south, the visitor begins his inspections of

THE EASTERN FRIEZE,

or those portions which decorated the eastern end of the Parthenon. These are marked from 17 to 24. The introductory slab (17) represents a procession of Greek virgins, with their long flowing draperies beautifully modelled, as the visitor will at once perceive. Some are carrying vessels for the libations. The next slab (18) has some interesting figures. The four standing figures, which are to the left of the two, supposed to represent Castor and Pollux, are supposed to represent Hierophants explaining away mysteries, while the others are students of the doctrines taught at the festival. The next slab, which is the longest in the collection (19), is said to have been originally placed above the eastern gate of the temple. Here are females delivering offerings in baskets to one who appears to preside. On the left, a man of dignified bearing is receiving a large roll from a youth, which Visconti supposed to be the embroidered veil. Here seated on a throne is Jupiter, with the arms supported by two sphinxes. Here, too, is a goddess removing her veil, supposed by some to be Juno, and by others Mercury. At the end of the slab the visitor will remark old AEsculapius, and the figure of his daughter with a serpent twined about her left arm, as Hygieia, or Health. The marble let into the wall below the frieze, and marked 20, is a perfect cast from a marble partly in that marked 21 and partly in that marked 22. Slabs 23, 24 have continuations of the procession, consisting of females draped, bearing vessels and torches. These women were selected from the noblest families of Athens. The fragment marked 25 closes those which adorn the eastern front. It represents a mutilated figure of one of the Metoeci, or strangers, bearing a tray filled originally with provisions. From the eastern the visitor should proceed to the slabs of the

NORTHERN FRIEZE.

These are marked from 26 to 46. On the first of this series a youth was originally represented receiving a crown of honour in a chariot race. Then follow successively five slabs, all bearing bas-reliefs of chariots and charioteers. These slabs are greatly admired by artists, and are said, at the present day, to be perhaps the finest specimens of bas-relief extant. After the chariots with more notable people forming the procession, the successive marbles marked 32 to 43 are filled up with the groups of horsemen who followed the chariots. The forms of the animals are beautifully grouped and executed; and may, after the many centuries of time that have elapsed since they were placed behind the Parthenon columns, be consulted by the modern artist as the finest extant models upon which he can exercise his student's hand. On the slabs 36, 7, how finely are the horses and riders grouped, and how firmly and gracefully is the rude figure upon the central horse of the second slab posed! Having sufficiently admired these fine groups, the visitor should at once turn to the slab marked 46. Here, a young man standing near his horse is about to crown himself; while a standing figure to the right appears to have dismounted, and to be suffering some adjustment of dress by a servant behind him. At the right end of this slab is a figure seen sideways, and representing the first part of the decoration of the

WESTERN FRIEZE.

Only one of the fifteen slabs of the western frieze is the original marble:--the rest are casts from the frieze still adorning the ruins of the temple. The western frieze is included in the slabs marked from 47 to 61. The marble in the possession of the museum from the western frieze is, however, one of great value. It represents two mounted horsemen--the whole exquisitely carved. Passing forward from this, the forty-eighth slab (48) represents a horse to which three men are attending. Mounted horsemen also fill up the next two slabs (49, 50). On the fifty-first a rider is represented habited in full armour, with another rider, dismounted, who appears to be rubbing a hurt on his left leg. The two following slabs (52,3) are horses and men;--on the latter, a dismounted man in a flowing robe endeavouring to curb a rearing steed. On the next slab (54) are two horsemen mounted, the one to the right wearing a hat that has a modern appearance, and is similar to those worn by dignitaries of the Greek church at the present time. A fine horse and graceful horseman occur in the right corner of the slab 55,--the action of the horse is finely sculptured. The remaining sculptures of the western frieze represent figures of mounted and dismounted horsemen, of which the visitor may notice the graceful figures on slab 57 (where the horse is rubbing his leg), and slab 60, where the figure to the right appears to be only preparing to join the procession. Having examined these, the visitor should at once proceed to examine the remarkable points of the

SOUTHERN FRIEZE.

These are numbered from 62 to 90, and reach back to the northern side of the entrance to the saloon. The slabs marked from 62 to 77 consist of horsemen, galloping, often two or three abreast: some with helmets and armour, and others nude; and the slabs marked from 78 to 82 have sculptures of chariots drawn by four horses (mostly) abreast. These, however, present no new points to which it is necessary to draw the visitor's particular attention. The business of the festival, &c., begins to be apparent in the seven last slabs (84-90). Here the victims appear. In the first (85) a bull appears to be giving no little trouble to some attendants, and to be utterly regardless of the solemnity of the occasion. A bull, full of action, is the principal object on the next slab (86): and on the next (87), one appears calmly walking to his doom. Upon the return of the slab (90) is a figure finely executed, supposed to be that of a magistrate surveying the progress of the procession. The sacrificial oxen are said to be masterly representations of the finest specimens of these animals.

Having examined these bas-reliefs, the visitor should at once turn to the groups which occupied central space in the saloon, and which originally adorned the eastern and western pediments of the Parthenon.

SCULPTURES FROM THE EASTERN PEDIMENT.

These occupy the central space towards the southern end of the saloon. The group on the eastern pediment originally represented the birth of Minerva. The visitor will probably be first attracted to the great recumbent figure marked 93, generally believed to have represented Theseus, the Athenian hero, whose biography opens the series of Plutarch's Lives. The figure is now much mutilated; the nose has been chipped, and the feet are wanting, but still the form reclining on a rock is majestic. Mr. Westmacott, in a lecture, gave his reasons for believing that this statue was meant for Cephalus, of whom Aurora was enamoured, and not Theseus. "This work [the pediment] it must be observed, related to the most remarkable event in Athenian mythology, and was confined only to that event. All the gods of Olympus were present at the birth of Minerva. Now Theseus was not only not in existence, but was patronised and protected by Minerva; it would seem, therefore, extraordinary that he should be admitted as a witness of her birth. If it is really Theseus, he could only have been introduced by Phidias in compliment to the Athenians; but whether this could on so very sacred an occasion have been allowed, may very reasonably be doubted. Hercules, even the older, or Idaean Hercules, was, upon the same principle, equally inadmissible, the Athenians acknowledging or worshipping no Hercules prior to the son of Alcmene, who was contemporaneous with Theseus, and consequently posterior also to Minerva. Now the mythology of Cephalus is not only in unison with Pausanias, but the admission of that person would in no degree affect the harmony of the Attic types, or principles of Athenian worship. Cephalus was as celebrated for heroic virtues as for his beauty."

The fragment numbered 91 is part of a figure of Hyperion rising out of the sea. It marked that angle of the pediment to the left of the spectator, and the arms are stretched forward urging his coursers. Near him are, alas, only the heads of two of his horses (92). The next group that presents itself for notice is that of two sitting figures (94), the one to the left leaning on the right shoulder of the other. This is a wreck of a group that represented Ceres and her daughter Proserpine on the pediment. Next in succession is a figure full of action (95): this is Iris, the messenger of the gods, but the particular property of Juno, on her way to carry to remote parts the interesting intelligence of the birth of Minerva. A torso of Victory is placed next in order of succession (96). The figure is now wingless, but holes can be seen which once attached them to the statue. Three Fates, beautifully draped (97), and a head of one of the horses (98) of the chariot of Night which occupied the angle of the pediment on the spectator's right, complete the recovered fragments of the eastern pediment.

Hence the visitor should turn to the fragments from the
WESTERN PEDIMENT.

The subject illustrated on the western pediment was the contest between Minerva and Neptune for the honour of giving a name to Athens. The relics of these sculptures will now engage the visitor's attention. Undoubtedly the first object that will attract his notice will be that numbered 99. This recumbent figure has a noble presence even now, headless and otherwise mutilated as it is. Canova stood undecided between this figure and that of Theseus (or Cephalus, according to Mr. Westmacott) as to which was pre-eminently beautiful. The figure before which the visitor now stands is generally received as the statue of Ilissus, who was the Athenian god of the river Ilissus, which watered the southern side of the Athenian plain. Others have declared it to be Theseus reposing after his herculean labours, and contemplating the contest between the two deities. Having fully examined this fine sculpture, the visitor should turn to the fragments of the Minerva. A small fragment of the upper part of a face (101) is all that remains of Minerva's head, the holes being still visible by which the goddess's bronze helmet was fastened to the statue. Hereabouts, also, is a fragment of the statue (102), and a coil of the serpent that was about the figure (104). The torso marked 100, from the western pediment, is conjectured to be part of a statue that represented Cecrops, the founder of Athens, at the contest. The next fragment is the torso of Neptune (103); and hereabouts is the cast of the group supposed to have originally represented Hercules and Hebe. The second object, marked 104, is the cast, presented by M. Charles Lenormand, of a head in the Bibliotheque Nationale at Paris, supposed to belong to one of the statues of the western pediment. A torso of a wingless or Athenian Victory is the next object that demands notice (105): the figure was represented without wings, in token of the inseparability of the goddess from the Greek capital. Another object is marked 105: this is the head of the Victory; or rather a cast from the original head presented to the trustees by Count de Laborde. Lastly, of the western pediment sculptures, the visitor will remark the lap of a figure, with a portion of an infant remaining: this ruin is all that is left of Latona and her two children, Diana and Apollo. Having fully examined these ruins of the Parthenon, the visitor must direct his immediate attention to the remains collected from the ruins of the celebrated

DOUBLE TEMPLE OF THE ERECTHEUM AND PANDROSUS.

The temple of the Erectheum was situated at Athens, less than two hundred feet distant from the Parthenon. It was the temple of Athene Polias, or Minerva and Erectheus; and adjoining it was the chapel of Pandrosus. Philocles of Acharnae was the architect of the building, which Lord Aberdeen, reiterating the opinion of many great authorities, in his "Inquiry into the Principles of Beauty in Grecian Architecture," styles the most perfect known specimen of the Ionic order of architecture. It was built on the spot where Neptune and Minerva are supposed to have contested the honour of naming Athens. When Lord Elgin visited Athens, the vestibule of the temple was a Turkish powder magazine.

Before examining the few relics from this fine building in the saloon, the visitor should notice the second object, marked 106, which is the cast of a head found during the progress of excavations at Athens, between the ancient gate of the Peloponnesus and the temple of Theseus. Having passed from this relic, the visitor will at once examine the architectural relics of different parts of the Erectheum, which are more interesting to the architectural student than to the general visitor. The fragment 109 is the lower portion of a draped female statue; the relic marked 110 is part of the shaft of an Ionic column; the capital of a column, 125, is very beautiful: but the object that will be most attractive to the general visitor is the statue marked 128, known in architecture as a Caryatid, which was used in the temple of Pandrosus instead of columns. Hereabouts also, amid the miscellaneous fragments, the visitor should notice a colossal headless and heavily-draped figure, marked 111. This is the wreck of the great statue of Bacchus which surmounted a monument erected three hundred and twenty years before the Christian era, by Thrasyllus of Deceleia, to record the victory of a tribe at a great festival of Bacchus. This statue has been variously christened. Some believe it to be the fragment of a Niobe; others of a Diana. It is generally allowed to be a noble sample of Greek sculpture. Hereabouts, also, is the well-known imperfect statue of Icarus (113), brought in fragments from the Acropolis. The urn marked 122 is a sepulchral vessel, with figures in bas-relief; 123 is a sepulchral column, with an Athenian name upon it; and then the visitor will pass rapidly the fragments of Doric and Ionic columns from various Greek temples. With the casts beginning from 136, the visitor will start with his examination of the fragments from the

TEMPLE OF THESEUS.

When the ashes of Theseus, long after his death, were conveyed in state to Athens, festivals were instituted in his honour; and a magnificent temple was erected to his memory nearly five centuries before our era. The sculptures of the temple represented the exploits of Theseus, and of Hercules, with whom Theseus was always on terms of great friendship, and to whom he gave the highest honours his country could afford. The subject of the frieze (which the visitor will find against the eastern wall of the saloon, numbered from 136 to 149), has been variously explained, but is shrewdly conjectured to be the Battle of the Giants, in which Hercules played a prominent part, and in which the giants are said to have hurled rocks at their adversaries, like pebbles. This battle was fought in the presence of divinities, who are represented seated upon slabs (137-8-133-4.) This frieze was on the most conspicuous part of the temple. The frieze that flanked the building was sculptured with the exploits of Theseus; and here the visitor will once more see the battle of the Centaurs and the Lapithae illustrated (150-154). The Centaurs hurling huge stones, and wielding the stems of trees; and the invulnerable Coeneus, half crushed by his savage enemies, are again represented. The casts of three metopes (155-157) are from the north side of the temple of Theseus. Upon the first the hero is represented destroying the King of Thebes, Creon; upon the second he is throwing Cercyon, King of Eleusis; and upon the third he is overcoming the Crommyonian sow. "About this time," Plutarch tells us, "Crommyon was infested with a wild sow named Phoeae, a fierce and formidable creature. This savage he attacked and killed, going out of his way to engage her, and thus displaying an act of voluntary valour: for he believed it equally became a brave man to stand upon his defence against abandoned ruffians, and to seek out and begin the combat with strong and savage animals. But some say that Phoeae was an abandoned female robber, who dwelt in Crommyon; that she had the name of 'sow' from her life and manners, and was afterwards slain by Theseus."

A series of bas-reliefs from an Ionic temple, dedicated to the Wingless Victory of Athens, are the next objects that command the general visitor's attention. They are numbered from 158 to 161 successively. Upon these are represented battles between the Greeks and Persians; and maidens leading a sacrificial bull. The fragments marked successively from 165 to 175 are remarkable for the Greek inscriptions on them, which cannot interest the general visitor. Let the visitor, therefore, next pause before the fragment of a frieze in green stone, marked 177, which is from the tomb of Agamemnon at Mycenae. The sculptured scroll-work is of very remote antiquity. The next fragment is a bas-relief, on which a bearded man is represented, pressing a child towards him, and directing its attention to a votive foot which he holds in his hand. Passing from this, the visitor may next direct his attention to the fragment of a colossal statue numbered 178. It belongs to one of the pediments of the Parthenon. Hereabouts are various sepulchral urns and columns of no particular interest to the casual observer;--the circular altar from Delos, ornamented in relief with sacrificial bulls and other subjects. 179 may, however, be noticed, together with the column marked 183, which bears the name of Socrates, son of Socrates, a native of Ancyra, of Galatia. The object marked 186 is a Greek sun-dial found at Athens, of a time not long before the reign of the Emperor Severus. Passing other altars and fragments of columns, the visitor should pause on his way, to notice a bas-relief upon which Latona and Diana are sculptured, forming part of a procession (190). The bas-relief numbered 193 is from the theatre of Bacchus: it is a Bacchanalian group, in which Bacchus is holding forth a vessel to be filled by an attending Bacchante. The next object to be noticed is marked 194, and is a fragment of a head of the goddess Pasht, surmounted with a crown of serpents. A spirited scene occurs upon bas-relief 197, where a charioteer, heralded by a flying Victory, is represented driving four horses at full speed. A series of urns and votive altars are grouped hereabouts, which the casual visitor may pass, pausing before the small statue of Ganymede (207); a fragment of a boy supporting a bird on his arm (221); a small figure of Telesphorus, headless, and draped; more sepulchral urns and steles; capitals of Corinthian and Ionic columns; various inscriptions, including a decree of a society of musicians (235); an amphora (238); a female head; a large and small head of a bearded Hercules (243-242); heads and fragments of heads; the base of a statue supposed to have been that of the Minerva of the western pediment of the Parthenon; urns and columns, and stales and inscriptions; a bas-relief showing Health, the daughter of Æsculapius, feeding a serpent; two more bas-reliefs; an inventory of the articles of gold and silver belonging to the Parthenon (282); steles, inscriptions, and columns; fragments of colossal statues, a small statue (headless) of a Muse, 316; fragments of figures from the metopes of the Parthenon; a sculptured oblong vessel, found near the plain of Troy, for containing holy water (324); a mutilated colossal head supposed to represent Nemesis, found in the temple of Nemesis, at Rhamnus (325); a mutilated female statue found also at Rhamnus, in the temple of Themis; fragments of colossal statues, steles, inscriptions, and altars. And hereabouts the visitor should pause once more to examine a consecutive series of sculptures. These are marked from 352 to 360. They are casts from the monument of Lysicrates, erected to celebrate a musical contest about three centuries and a half before our era. This monument is commonly known as the

LANTERN OF DEMOSTHENES.

This name is derived from a story long current, that the monument was built by Demosthenes as a place of retirement. It was in reality a monument erected in honour of Lysicrates, and the musicians or actors who carried off the palm in musical or dramatic entertainments. This monument is interesting as being the oldest existing specimen of the Corinthian order of architecture. The frieze, of which there are specimens before the visitor, represents the story of the revenge Bacchus indulged in towards some Tyrrhenian corsairs, who endeavoured to convey him to Asia to sell him as a slave. It is related that discovering their infamous project, he transformed the masts and oars of the vessel into snakes. The frieze is divided into nine compartments, and the central figure is Bacchus seated with his panther before him, a vessel in his hand, and attendant fauns. The fantastic punishment of the pirates is forcibly depicted. Here one bound to a rock finds the cord changed into a powerful serpent; there men leaping into the sea are already half changed to dolphins; and others are receiving severe castigation. Having examined these curious sculptures, the visitor may rapidly review the rest of the relics which he will care to examine. Passing the inscriptions (all interesting to the antiquarian), the votive altars, and other fragments, he may halt here and there before various interesting bas-reliefs. Among these are a bas-relief representing Vesta and Minerva crowning a young man (375); a bas-relief of Jupiter and Juno; a bas-relief representing a sacrifice before an altar (380); an imperfect bas-relief representing three goddesses (383); a lion's head from the roof of the Parthenon (393); a fragment from Mantell's collection, of a female figure found on the plains of Marathon (397); the upper part of a female figure, in bas-relief, from Athens (419); two women and a child making offerings found in Laconia (430); another bas-relief from Laconia (431); a curious subject in bas-relief from Athens, representing the upper part of a youth holding something, supposed to be a lantern, with a boy near him, and a cat on a column (432); a cast from a tablet representing in bas-relief Pan seated on a rock with a draped nymph, supposed to be Echo, before him (433); a cast of the tablet of Euthydia, daughter of Diogenes, who is taking leave of friends (435); and lastly, a bas-relief representing the shape of a shield, on which the names of the *ephebi* of Athens, under Alcamenes, are inscribed. This is said to have belonged originally to the Parthenon. And here the visitor will close his inspection of the Elgin Saloon. That he will return to these fine relics of the old Greeks, if he have the opportunity, is certain. He may come again and again, and each time gain something in the contemplation of these classical models; noble thoughts before the masterly figure of Theseus, a keen sense of beauty near the beautiful forms of the Parthenon frieze. Of all the glorious monuments of antiquity that have reached us of the proud nineteenth century, none have so noble a significance as the broken marbles collected in this room. The contemplative man, seeing their perfect beauties, asks himself in their presence many puzzling questions. But perhaps the first that rises in the mind is wonder at the contrast between the development of art and the poorness of science in this splendid antiquity. No steam then to wield the hammer; only the most limited knowledge of the earth: the west an indescribable region of harmony and glory; the world a flat surface; fearful mariners hugging the shore close at home, and trusting to the stars; and England a savage place where wolves rent the air at night; and a heathen mythology the faith of the most civilised people of the earth. Under these barbarous circumstances, the poetry that dwells in the heart of all people who cultivate some affinity to nature, fashioned the mould of a Phidias for the people of Athens. A man with a stern soul, an eye large and grand, a frame built to realise the soul's tasks--we see this Phidias of the Greeks as he hovered about the foundations of the Parthenon, when the name of Pericles was every Greek's watchword, four centuries and a half before our Christian era. The man appears to have been of colossal parts in every way. Versed in history, a poet given to study fables (as all poets are), keen in sifting the subtleties of geometry, a passionate reader of Homer; this was indeed the sculptor of the gods! Of the high estimation in which the sculptures of the Parthenon should be held, it is superfluous to say more than all writers on art have agreed in saying. Here we have master-pieces, beyond which the sculptors of the many ages that have passed away since Phidias laboured at his Jupiter in the Olympian grove have never reached. High praise this to say of a man who has been twenty-two centuries in his grave, that he accomplished in the utmost perfection those ideals to which his imitators have vainly aspired. It appears that Phidias had his troubles, knew the force of a frown from men in power, and in exile produced his master-piece. Whether he died in disgrace and by foul means are points upon which the dust of ages has settled for ever. We know thus much of him and no more. But the visitor who has probably been more impressed with the contents of the Elgin Saloon than with the massive coarseness of the Egyptian antiquities, will be glad to hear a few general words--an authoritative summing up of the matter from a pen more clearly authorised to touch the subject than ours can be. A brief summary, a terse description, analytical and picturesque, of a field of speculation or a region of wonder, systematises the spectator's impression, and with the view of fastening the proper contemplation of these master-pieces upon the visitor's mind, we quote a few pointed sentences on the sculptures of the Elgin Saloon, from the pen of Sir Henry Ellis.

"These marbles, chiefly ornamental, belong to one edifice dedicated to the guardian deity of the city, raised at the time of the greatest political power of the state, when all the arts which contribute to humanise life were developing their beneficial influence. Many of the writers of Athens, whose works are the daily text-books of our schools, saw in their original perfection the mutilated marbles which we still cherish and admire. The Elgin collection has presented us with the external and material forms, in which the art of Phidias gave life and reality to the beautiful mythi which veiled the origin of his native city, and perpetuated in groups of matchless simplicity the ceremonies of the great national festival. The lover of beauty and the friend of Grecian learning will here find a living comment on what he reads; and as in the best and severest models of antiquity we always discover something new to admire, so here we find fresh beauties at every visit, and learn how infinite in variety are simplicity and truth, and how every deviation from these principles produces sameness and satiety. It is but just that those who feel the value of this collection should pay a tribute of thanks to the nobleman to whose exertions the nation is indebted for it; and the more so as he was made the object of vulgar abuse by many pretended admirers of ancient learning. If Lord Elgin had not removed these marbles, there is no doubt that many of them would long since have been totally destroyed; and it was only after great hesitation, and a certain knowledge that they were daily suffering more and more from brutal ignorance and barbarism, that he could prevail on himself to employ the power he had obtained to remove them to England. These marbles may be considered in two ways; first, as mere specimens of sculpture; and secondly, as forming part of the history of a people. As specimens of sculpture they serve as excellent studies to young artists, whose taste is formed and chastened by the simplicity and truth of the models presented to them. The advantage of studying the ancients in this department of art rests pretty nearly on the same grounds as those which may be given for our study of their written models. Modern times produce excellence in every department of human industry, and our knowledge of nature, the result of continued accumulations, needs not now the limited experience of former ages. The sciences founded on demonstration, though they may trace their origin to the writings of the Greeks, have advanced to a state in which nothing would be gained by constantly recurring to the ancient condition of knowledge. But it is not so with those arts which belong to the province of design; they require a different discipline, and the faculties which they employ may have received a more complete development two thousand years ago, under favourable circumstances, than they have now. Their perfection depends on circumstances over which we have little control: they cannot, in our opinion, ever become essentially popular in any country but one where the climate favours an out-of-door life, and where they are intimately blended in the service of religion. If then a nation has existed whose physical organisation, whose climate, and whose religion all combined to develop the principles of beauty, and taught man to choose from nature those forms and combinations which give the highest and most lasting pleasure, we of the present day who do not possess these advantages must follow those who were the first true interpreters of nature. Their models possess the advantage of being fixed; for without some standard universally admitted, we should run into all the extravagances of conceit and affectation.

"No work of the present time is ever universally admitted as an indisputable standard. It is only when time has placed an interval between the present and the past, wide enough to destroy all the rivalries of competition; that great works receive the full acknowledgments of their merits, and become standards to which we all appeal. Thus in the art of writing our own language, we refer to the best models of past instead of to the works of our own days; and our youth at school are chiefly trained on the written models of Greece and Home, instead of those of our own country. The advantage of this consists in having before us examples which all appeal to, not because we contend that they are in all respects the best, but because they were the best of their day, and being written in a language no longer subject to change, may be taken as an universal standard by which all civilised nations may measure their thoughts and the mode of expressing them. The frieze of the Parthenon and the dramas of Sophocles, the forms of the marble and the conceptions of the great poet, still speak to our imagination and our understanding: we recognise, in both, the beauty of proportion, the simplicity and truth of design; and we all assent to a standard which we feel to be in harmony with nature, and to which all nations will yield a more ready obedience than to any other that we can name.

"Though the artist and the student may examine the sculptures of the Parthenon with somewhat different views, their studies are more nearly allied than is generally supposed. The artist who looks at them merely as delineations of form, without reference to the ideas which gave them their existence, loses half the pleasure and the profit; and the student who merely names and catalogues them, without connecting them with the written monuments of Grecian genius, that is with the illustration of ancient texts, is also pursuing a barren study."

And now the visitor's way lies through the sculpture galleries, back to the grand entrance. He has accomplished the labour of examining all that is exhibited to the public generally of the contents of the national museum. He may wander into the eastern wing of the building (if it be open to the general visitor), and through the northern, where the vast library of printed books and manuscripts are deposited; but these are only accessible to the public under special regulations. This remark is applicable also to the print-room.

The visitor, however, cannot leave the British Museum, having wandered over it and examined its various curiosities, without getting something from his journey. It is full of suggestive matter, which, with a little direction, may be turned to useful account by large classes of the people. It affords glimpses into the mysteries of the Animal Kingdom, with all its varieties, its wonders, its traceable progresses, its past and extinct forms, its promises of future developments. Then the mineralogical galleries afford the general visitor a peep at the formations of the earth; the various developments of minerals; the natural state of ores and stones which most men see only in their manufactured state. From the mineralogical tables the visitor stepped aside to examine the wondrous revelations of extinct animal life recovered from the bowels of the earth; he saw the colossal megatherium, the towering mastodon, and the great Irish elk. He understood something of the progress of animal life, from the fishes and the saurians. Then he passed into the Egyptian room, and found himself surrounded with the preserved bodies of the ancient Egyptians; he examined their household gods; he pried into their coffins; he saw their food; he was familiarised with their apparel. Still proceeding onward, he came to the beautiful bronzes; and then he saw the wonders that the ancient tombs of Etruria disgorged. He still advanced in the galleries, till he came to a room that was a little museum in itself--an exhibition of the curious industries of many different countries. Here were Buddhist temples; Chinese chopsticks; marvels from savage islands; a tortoise-shell bonnet; a Chinese bell;--in short, a room packed from the ceiling to the floor with a compact mass of curiosities. And then he left the upper floor of the building, after having spent two days there, through two towering cameleopards. He came a third time, and at once passing many things that tempted him by the way, he passed on into the great and wonderful Egyptian Saloon. Here he lingered for hours over ancient Egyptian tombstones; before colossal sarcophagi; thinking of the tough work Belzoni must have had of it with the young Memnon; endeavouring to realise the approach to the ancient Egyptian temples through rows of colossal and majestic sphinxes. Next he passed on to the ruins of Nineveh, and its mystic mounds. Here he was with Layard for a time, dreaming of the ancient Assyrians and their winged bulls. Hence he passed into the Lycian room, and saw something of the strange remains of the Xanthus of old; and then, probably, he went home to dream of these great marvels of the times gone by. But he came again; and this time hovered throughout the day amid the ruins of the arts of ancient Greece. And now he has examined these; and he may leave the national museum, assured that he has some useful knowledge of the curiosities which scientific men have gathered from the remote parts of the world, for the benefit of the learned resident in England.

The tens of thousands who flock to the museum in holiday times prove its attractions; and it is with the hope that these attractions may be enhanced by the help of a methodical and homely guide, chattering to the visitor various bits and scraps of pertinent information as he passes from one object to another, that these four visits have been presented to the public. They do not pretend to be scientific books, but simply companions of the hour, that urge little points of information while the mind is particularly impressible; and showing the kind of interest that attaches to objects which, for the want of a timely word, the visitor would have passed unnoticed.

Many objects which are curiosities to the scientific man, but which could not in any way interest the casual visitor, have been passed by without hesitation.

Our main object has been to give the visitor clear impressions of the different departments or classes into which the national collection naturally divides itself, by guiding his eye consecutively to those objects which bear relation to each other. It was necessary, to make ourselves attractive as guides, to eschew all learned and stiff formalities; to class matters easily as we found them; and to sustain the visitor's interest throughout his four journeys. The monotony of a formal catalogue is repulsive to visitors chiefly bent upon enjoying a few hours amusement; therefore we chose to direct the eye to objects, and at once to interest the visitor in them, by shortly explaining their points of interest. The success which this endeavour met elsewhere has encouraged us to perform the present task; and we hope shortly to be at the elbow of visitors to other interesting buildings and exhibitions.

The popularity of the British Museum may be shown by quoting the last return of the number of visitors, &c., presented to the House of Commons. This return proves that, while the public interest in the collection is on the increase, that the guardians of the different departments look out eagerly for new curiosities:--"The number of readers--or rather of visits made by readers, in 1850, was 78,533:--or, an average of some 268 per diem:--the Reading Rooms having been kept open 291 days. The number of books returned to the shelves of the General Library from the Reading Rooms was 119,093; to those of the Royal Library, 11,252; to those of the Grenville Library, 387: to the closets in which the books are kept from day to day for the use of the readers, 110,950:--making a total of 241,682, or 830 per diem. The number of volumes added to the Library amounts to 16,208 (including music, maps, and newspapers); of which 837 were presented, 11,793 purchased, and 3575 received by copyright. The Keeper of the MSS. has been busy cleaning, cataloguing, and stamping. Eleven of the valuable Cottonian MSS. on vellum (including the Chronicle of Roger de Wendover, supposed to have been utterly destroyed), and two Old Royal as well as five Cottonian on paper, all injured in the fire of 1731, have been carefully repaired, inlaid, and rebound. The purchases include a Psalter of the tenth century, formerly belonging to the monastery of Stavelot, in the diocese of Liege,--'a remarkably fine Greek MS.' containing the works ascribed to Dionysius the Areopagite,--and the Homilies of Gregory of Nazianzum, 'with scholia written in the year 6480 (A.D. 972);'--together with nineteen additional volumes of a series of transcripts from the Archives at the Hague, of documents relating to English history, extending from 1588 to 1614 and from 1689 to 1702.--In the 'Department of Natural History,' we find that great progress has been made in the arrangement of the contents of Room No. VI.,--its wall cases having been entirely filled with the gigantic Osseous Remains of Edentata and Pachydermata, and that the Central Room of the Northern Zoological Gallery has been devoted to a collection of the Beasts, Birds, Fish, Reptiles, Shells, Sea Eggs, Starfish, and Corals found in the British Islands. The purchases include 'a silver decadrachm of Alexander the Great,' from the collection of Colonel Rawlinson,--the first ever discovered,--'and two very rare British *gold* coins, having on them the name TIN.'"

NOTES

[1: Undoubtedly the finest coral is dredged from the Mediterranean; it is an important article of commerce at Marseilles.]

[2: "The shrikes, or butcher-birds (laniadae), are a numerous and widely-diffused assemblage, living upon the smaller birds and insects; the former of which the shrike sticks, when killed, upon thorns, as a butcher hangs up meat in his stall; hence the name of the genus."--Vestiges of Creation.]

[3: Vestiges of Creation.]

[4: These birds build in the crevices of precipitous rocks, and tho female lines the nest with the down plucked from her breast. From these nests natives rob the down and sell it.]

[5: Vestiges of Creation.]

[6: "Oxides are neutral compounds, containing oxygen in equivalent proportions."--Dr. Ure.]

[7: Sesquicarbonate of soda that is found in the west of the Delta. In Mexico there are several natron lakes.]

[8: The cuneiform character, which was used in every part of Asia Minor, up to the time of Alexander the Great, consists of a series of wedges or accents variously combined, as, [Cuneiform: *** **]].

[9: A Metope may be described as the intermediate space in a Doric frieze, between two triglyphs, or separating grooves.]

www.bookjungle.com email: sales@bookjungle.com fax: 630-214-0564 mail: Book Jungle PO Box 2226 Champaign, IL 61825

The Codes Of Hammurabi And Moses
W. W. Davies

QTY

The discovery of the Hammurabi Code is one of the greatest achievements of archaeology, and is of paramount interest, not only to the student of the Bible, but also to all those interested in ancient history...

Religion   ISBN: *1-59462-338-4*   Pages:132
MSRP $12.95

The Theory of Moral Sentiments
Adam Smith

QTY

This work from 1749. contains original theories of conscience amd moral judgment and it is the foundation for systemof morals.

Philosophy   ISBN: *1-59462-777-0*   Pages:536
MSRP $19.95

Jessica's First Prayer
Hesba Stretton

QTY

In a screened and secluded corner of one of the many railway-bridges which span the streets of London there could be seen a few years ago, from five o'clock every morning until half past eight, a tidily set-out coffee-stall, consisting of a trestle and board, upon which stood two large tin cans, with a small fire of charcoal burning under each so as to keep the coffee boiling during the early hours of the morning when the work-people were thronging into the city on their way to their daily toil...

Childrens   ISBN: *1-59462-373-2*   Pages:84
MSRP $9.95

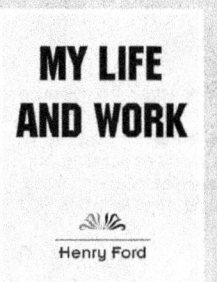

My Life and Work
Henry Ford

QTY

Henry Ford revolutionized the world with his implementation of mass production for the Model T automobile. Gain valuable business insight into his life and work with his own auto-biography... "We have only started on our development of our country we have not as yet, with all our talk of wonderful progress, done more than scratch the surface. The progress has been wonderful enough but..."

Biographies/   ISBN: *1-59462-198-5*   **Pages:300**
MSRP $21.95

www.bookjungle.com email: sales@bookjungle.com fax: 630-214-0564 mail: Book Jungle PO Box 2226 Champaign, IL 61825

The Art of Cross-Examination
Francis Wellman

QTY

I presume it is the experience of every author, after his first book is published upon an important subject, to be almost overwhelmed with a wealth of ideas and illustrations which could readily have been included in his book, and which to his own mind, at least, seem to make a second edition inevitable. Such certainly was the case with me; and when the first edition had reached its sixth impression in five months, I rejoiced to learn that it seemed to my publishers that the book had met with a sufficiently favorable reception to justify a second and considerably enlarged edition. ...

Reference   ISBN: *1-59462-647-2*   Pages:412   MSRP $19.95

On the Duty of Civil Disobedience
Henry David Thoreau

QTY

Thoreau wrote his famous essay, On the Duty of Civil Disobedience, as a protest against an unjust but popular war and the immoral but popular institution of slave-owning. He did more than write—he declined to pay his taxes, and was hauled off to gaol in consequence. Who can say how much this refusal of his hastened the end of the war and of slavery ?

Law   ISBN: *1-59462-747-9*   Pages:48   MSRP $7.45

Dream Psychology Psychoanalysis for Beginners
Sigmund Freud

QTY

Sigmund Freud, born Sigismund Schlomo Freud (May 6, 1856 - September 23, 1939), was a Jewish-Austrian neurologist and psychiatrist who co-founded the psychoanalytic school of psychology. Freud is best known for his theories of the unconscious mind, especially involving the mechanism of repression; his redefinition of sexual desire as mobile and directed towards a wide variety of objects; and his therapeutic techniques, especially his understanding of transference in the therapeutic relationship and the presumed value of dreams as sources of insight into unconscious desires.

Psychology   ISBN: *1-59462-905-6*   Pages:196   MSRP $15.45

The Miracle of Right Thought
Orison Swett Marden

QTY

Believe with all of your heart that you will do what you were made to do. When the mind has once formed the habit of holding cheerful, happy, prosperous pictures, it will not be easy to form the opposite habit. It does not matter how improbable or how far away this realization may see, or how dark the prospects may be, if we visualize them as best we can, as vividly as possible, hold tenaciously to them and vigorously struggle to attain them, they will gradually become actualized, realized in the life. But a desire, a longing without endeavor, a yearning abandoned or held indifferently will vanish without realization.

Self Help   ISBN: *1-59462-644-8*   Pages:360   MSRP $25.45

www.bookjungle.com email: sales@bookjungle.com fax: 630-214-0564 mail: Book Jungle PO Box 2226 Champaign, IL 61825

QTY

QTY	Title	ISBN	Price
☐	**The Rosicrucian Cosmo-Conception Mystic Christianity** *by Max Heindel* The Rosicrucian Cosmo-conception is not dogmatic, neither does it appeal to any other authority than the reason of the student. It is: not controversial, but is: sent forth in the, hope that it may help to clear... *New Age/Religion Pages 646*	ISBN: *1-59462-188-8*	**$38.95**
☐	**Abandonment To Divine Providence** *by Jean-Pierre de Caussade* "The Rev. Jean Pierre de Caussade was one of the most remarkable spiritual writers of the Society of Jesus in France in the 18th Century. His death took place at Toulouse in 1751. His works have gone through many editions and have been republished... *Inspirational/Religion Pages 400*	ISBN: *1-59462-228-0*	**$25.95**
☐	**Mental Chemistry** *by Charles Haanel* Mental Chemistry allows the change of material conditions by combining and appropriately utilizing the power of the mind. Much like applied chemistry creates something new and unique out of careful combinations of chemicals the mastery of mental chemistry... *New Age Pages 354*	ISBN: *1-59462-192-6*	**$23.95**
☐	**The Letters of Robert Browning and Elizabeth Barret Barrett 1845-1846 vol II** *by Robert Browning and Elizabeth Barrett* *Biographies Pages 596*	ISBN: *1-59462-193-4*	**$35.95**
☐	**Gleanings In Genesis (volume I)** *by Arthur W. Pink* Appropriately has Genesis been termed "the seed plot of the Bible" for in it we have, in germ form, almost all of the great doctrines which are afterwards fully developed in the books of Scripture which follow... *Religion/Inspirational Pages 420*	ISBN: *1-59462-130-6*	**$27.45**
☐	**The Master Key** *by L. W. de Laurence* In no branch of human knowledge has there been a more lively increase of the spirit of research during the past few years than in the study of Psychology, Concentration and Mental Discipline. The requests for authentic lessons in Thought Control, Mental Discipline and... *New Age/Business Pages 422*	ISBN: *1-59462-001-6*	**$30.95**
☐	**The Lesser Key Of Solomon Goetia** *by L. W. de Laurence* This translation of the first book of the "Lernegton" which is now for the first time made accessible to students of Talismanic Magic was done, after careful collation and edition, from numerous Ancient Manuscripts in Hebrew, Latin, and French... *New Age/Occult Pages 92*	ISBN: *1-59462-092-X*	**$9.95**
☐	**Rubaiyat Of Omar Khayyam** *by Edward Fitzgerald* Edward Fitzgerald, whom the world has already learned, in spite of his own efforts to remain within the shadow of anonymity, to look upon as one of the rarest poets of the century, was born at Bredfield, in Suffolk, on the 31st of March, 1809. He was the third son of John Purcell... *Music Pages 172*	ISBN:*1-59462-332-5*	**$13.95**
☐	**Ancient Law** *by Henry Maine* The chief object of the following pages is to indicate some of the earliest ideas of mankind, as they are reflected in Ancient Law, and to point out the relation of those ideas to modern thought. *Religion/History Pages 452*	ISBN: *1-59462-128-4*	**$29.95**
☐	**Far-Away Stories** *by William J. Locke* "Good wine needs no bush, but a collection of mixed vintages does. And this book is just such a collection. Some of the stories I do not want to remain buried for ever in the museum files of dead magazine-numbers an author's not unpardonable vanity..." *Fiction Pages 272*	ISBN: *1-59462-129-2*	**$19.45**
☐	**Life of David Crockett** *by David Crockett* "Colonel David Crockett was one of the most remarkable men of the times in which he lived. Born in humble life, but gifted with a strong will, an indomitable courage, and unremitting perseverance... *Biographies/New Age Pages 424*	ISBN: *1-59462-250-7*	**$27.45**
☐	**Lip-Reading** *by Edward Nitchie* Edward B. Nitchie, founder of the New York School for the Hard of Hearing, now the Nitchie School of Lip-Reading, Inc, wrote "LIP-READING Principles and Practice". The development and perfecting of this meritorious work on lip-reading was an undertaking... *How-to Pages 400*	ISBN: *1-59462-206-X*	**$25.95**
☐	**A Handbook of Suggestive Therapeutics, Applied Hypnotism, Psychic Science** *by Henry Munro* *Health/New Age/Health/Self-help Pages 376*	ISBN: *1-59462-214-0*	**$24.95**
☐	**A Doll's House: and Two Other Plays** *by Henrik Ibsen* Henrik Ibsen created this classic when in revolutionary 1848 Rome. Introducing some striking concepts in playwriting for the realist genre, this play has been studied the world over. *Fiction/Classics/Plays 308*	ISBN: *1-59462-112-8*	**$19.95**
☐	**The Light of Asia** *by sir Edwin Arnold* In this poetic masterpiece, Edwin Arnold describes the life and teachings of Buddha. The man who was to become known as Buddha to the world was born as Prince Gautama of India but he rejected the worldly riches and abandoned the reigns of power when... *Religion/History/Biographies Pages 170*	ISBN: *1-59462-204-3*	**$13.95**
☐	**The Complete Works of Guy de Maupassant** *by Guy de Maupassant* "For days and days, nights and nights, I had dreamed of that first kiss which was to consecrate our engagement, and I knew not on what spot I should put my lips..." *Fiction/Classics Pages 240*	ISBN: *1-59462-157-8*	**$16.95**
☐	**The Art of Cross-Examination** *by Francis L. Wellman* Written by a renowned trial lawyer, Wellman imparts his experience and uses case studies to explain how to use psychology to extract desired information through questioning. *How-to/Science/Reference Pages 408*	ISBN: *1-59462-309-0*	**$26.95**
☐	**Answered or Unanswered?** *by Louisa Vaughan* Miracles of Faith in China *Religion Pages 112*	ISBN: *1-59462-248-5*	**$10.95**
☐	**The Edinburgh Lectures on Mental Science (1909)** *by Thomas* This book contains the substance of a course of lectures recently given by the writer in the Queen Street Hail, Edinburgh. Its purpose is to indicate the Natural Principles governing the relation between Mental Action and Material Conditions... *New Age/Psychology Pages 148*	ISBN: *1-59462-008-3*	**$11.95**
☐	**Ayesha** *by H. Rider Haggard* Verily and indeed it is the unexpected that happens! Probably if there was one person upon the earth from whom the Editor of this, and of a certain previous history, did not expect to hear again... *Classics Pages 380*	ISBN: *1-59462-301-5*	**$24.95**
☐	**Ayala's Angel** *by Anthony Trollope* The two girls were both pretty, but Lucy who was twenty-one who supposed to be simple and comparatively unattractive, whereas Ayala was credited, as her Bombwhat romantic name might show, with poetic charm and a taste for romance. Ayala when her father died was nineteen... *Fiction Pages 484*	ISBN: *1-59462-352-X*	**$29.95**
☐	**The American Commonwealth** *by James Bryce* An interpretation of American democratic political theory. It examines political mechanics and society from the perspective of Scotsman James Bryce *Politics Pages 572*	ISBN: *1-59462-286-8*	**$34.45**
☐	**Stories of the Pilgrims** *by Margaret P. Pumphrey* This book explores pilgrims religious oppression in England as well as their escape to Holland and eventual crossing to America on the Mayflower, and their early days in New England... *History Pages 268*	ISBN: *1-59462-116-0*	**$17.95**

www.bookjungle.com email: sales@bookjungle.com fax: 630-214-0564 mail: Book Jungle PO Box 2226 Champaign, IL 61825

			QTY
The Fasting Cure *by Sinclair Upton* In the Cosmopolitan Magazine for May, 1910, and in the Contemporary Review (London) for April, 1910, I published an article dealing with my experiences in fasting. I have written a great many magazine articles, but never one which attracted so much attention...	ISBN: *1-59462-222-1* New Age/Self Help/Health Pages 164	**$13.95**	☐
Hebrew Astrology *by Sepharial* In these days of advanced thinking it is a matter of common observation that we have left many of the old landmarks behind and that we are now pressing forward to greater heights and to a wider horizon than that which represented the mind-content of our progenitors...	ISBN: *1-59462-308-2* Astrology Pages 144	**$13.45**	☐
Thought Vibration or The Law of Attraction in the Thought World *by William Walker Atkinson*	ISBN: *1-59462-127-6* Psychology/Religion Pages 144	**$12.95**	☐
Optimism *by Helen Keller* Helen Keller was blind, deaf, and mute since 19 months old, yet famously learned how to overcome these handicaps, communicate with the world, and spread her lectures promoting optimism. An inspiring read for everyone...	ISBN: *1-59462-108-X* Biographies/Inspirational Pages 84	**$15.95**	☐
Sara Crewe *by Frances Burnett* In the first place, Miss Minchin lived in London. Her home was a large, dull, tall one, in a large, dull square, where all the houses were alike, and all the sparrows were alike, and where all the door-knockers made the same heavy sound...	ISBN: *1-59462-360-0* Childrens/Classic Pages 88	**$9.45**	☐
The Autobiography of Benjamin Franklin *by Benjamin Franklin* The Autobiography of Benjamin Franklin has probably been more extensively read than any other American historical work, and no other book of its kind has had such ups and downs of fortune. Franklin lived for many years in England, where he was agent...	ISBN: *1-59462-135-7* Biographies/History Pages 332	**$24.95**	☐

Name	
Email	
Telephone	
Address	
City, State ZIP	

☐ Credit Card   ☐ Check / Money Order

Credit Card Number	
Expiration Date	
Signature	

Please Mail to: Book Jungle
                   PO Box 2226
                   Champaign, IL 61825
or Fax to: 630-214-0564

ORDERING INFORMATION

web: *www.bookjungle.com*
email: *sales@bookjungle.com*
fax: *630-214-0564*
mail: *Book Jungle PO Box 2226 Champaign, IL 61825*
or PayPal *to sales@bookjungle.com*

Please contact us for bulk discounts

DIRECT-ORDER TERMS

20% Discount if You Order Two or More Books
Free Domestic Shipping!
Accepted: Master Card, Visa, Discover, American Express

www.ingramcontent.com/pod-product-compliance
Lightning Source LLC
Chambersburg PA
CBHW080508110426
42742CB00017B/3037